THE BUGABOO REVIEW

SUE SOMMER

THE BUGABOO REVIEW

A LIGHTHEARTED GUIDE TO EXTERMINATING CONFUSION ABOUT WORDS, SPELLING, AND GRAMMAR

New World Library
Novato, California

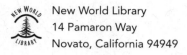

New World Library
14 Pamaron Way
Novato, California 94949

Text design by Tracy Cunningham
Cover and interior illustrations by Hannah Morris

Library of Congress Cataloging-in-Publication Data
Sommer, Sue.
 The bugaboo review : a lighthearted guide to exterminating confusion about words, spelling, and grammer / written and compiled by Sue Sommer.
     p.   cm.
ISBN 978-1-60868-026-9 (pbk. : alk. paper)
1. English language—Usage. 2. English language—Errors of usage.
3. English language—Grammar. 4. English language—Orthography and spelling. I. Title.
PE1460.S63 2011
428.2—dc23   2011018458

First printing, August 2011
ISBN 978-1-60868-026-9
Printed in Canada on 100% postconsumer-waste recycled paper

New World Library is a proud member of the Green Press Initiative.

10 9 8 7 6 5 4 3 2 1

CONTENTS

INTRODUCTION   VII

THE PARTS OF SPEECH   1

THE WORST OFFENDERS
The Bugs That Really Bite   5

THE BODY OF THE BUG   17

THE "EI" AND "IE" SECTION
These Words Are Just Waiting to Bite You   201

THE FINAL STINGERS
Commonly Misspelled Words   203

AFTERWORD
The Closing Buzz   207

ABOUT THE AUTHOR   209

INTRODUCTION

Bugaboo is from the archaic term *bogy boo* — a term for a hobgoblin or anything that haunts, bothers, bugs, harasses, irks, annoys, or frightens, like the bogeyman. *The Bugaboo Review* is a lighthearted examination of usage, grammar, and spelling mistakes, the bugaboos of the English language. It is meant for those who love language, for those who "know what they don't know" (or don't remember!), and for those in the process of learning English. My sources for this work range from errors made by my students, to suggestions by colleagues and friends who asked me to include errors that "bug" them, to discourses found in many other books, dictionaries, and articles on the subject.

The corrections recommended in this book mainly pertain to *formal* writing and speaking, but they also apply to everyday dialogue. The issues are listed in alphabetical order (after the "Worst Offenders" section in the beginning of the text). Words that are tricky to spell act as subheadings, often with the problem area underlined. I've explained some of these with a whimsical hint or trick to help you remember the problem areas. Those in the "Worst Offenders" category are repeated in the main list so they really sink in. Subheadings enclosed in quotation marks demonstrate incorrect spellings, with the corrections following. Italicized subheadings feature interesting items that don't quite fit into any particular category.

I hope you'll find this book entertaining and easy to use. I've left out the copious regulations that govern spellings and word usage and instead have given simple ideas to assist you with what is generally accepted among the well informed. This is a quick reference that lists some of the most common grammar pitfalls. It doesn't dig into intricate explanations. To learn more about any particular entry in *The Bugaboo Review*, I suggest that you consult the *Modern Language Association Handbook* or *The Chicago Manual of Style*. A few of the issues may be debatable because of our ever-altering language and communication habits, and some readers may take issue with portions of the *Bug-Rev*, as my students call it, but this broadly eclectic guide has proven to be a most helpful document. My young scholars save their copy when they leave high school and head to college, their parents often request their own copies, and my friends keep the *Bug-Rev* available for easy and rapid reference. I hope you will do the same, and enjoy the explanations along the way.

Yours in exterminating bugaboos,

SUE SOMMER

THE PARTS OF SPEECH

*H*ere is a quick reference guide to the parts of speech in the English language. I speak of these throughout *The Bugaboo Review*, so you may use this to refer to them.

Verb

Function: Indicates **action** or **state of being**.

Examples: spend, drive, see, dance, are, was, is, be, am.

Noun

Function: Names a **person**, **place**, **thing**, **idea**, or **activity**.

Examples: John Smith, Cher, home, church, hope, gentleness, freedom, tennis, badminton.

Pronoun

Function: Takes the **place of a noun**.

Examples: I, my, you, he, she, us, him, them, mine, myself, ours, who, your, it, they, anyone, that, which, who, any.

Adjective

Function: Describes a **noun** or **pronoun**.

Examples: hungry, rich, kind, jolly, old, solid, ugly, feasible, desperate, neat, whimsical.

Adverb

Function: Describes a **verb**, an **adjective**, or another **adverb**; it tells **when**, **how**, **where**, **why**, **under what conditions**, and **to what degree** things are done.

Examples: often, quietly, too, cheerfully, really, quite, normally, rarely, oddly, very, much, lightly.

Preposition

Function: Always followed by a noun or pronoun, called the object of the preposition, thus forming a prepositional phrase, often with an adjective or article. The preposition shows the relation to a verb, an adjective, or another noun or pronoun in the sentence. Prepositional phrases show *cause*, *amount*, *manner*, *place*, *time*, and *direction* (CAMPTD!).

Examples of prepositions: into, from, to, against, without, with, above, at, about, around, between, beyond, onto, across, but, barring, of, after, off, during, for, up, until, over, under, beneath.

Examples of prepositional phrases: for me; to you; toward the future; behind the yellow door; by the way; off the wall; through the roof; over the red line; by the sleepy lagoon; under the dirty, greasy, oil-leaking car; by the dawn's early light.

Conjunction

Function: Links or joins *words*, *phrases*, or *clauses*.

Examples: and, but, or, after, until, however. Note that some words, such as *but* and *until*, can be both conjunctions and prepositions; a preposition, however, MUST be followed by a noun or pronoun.

Interjection

Function: Shows surprise or emotion and is almost always followed by an exclamation point!

Examples: Oh! Ah! Wow! Hey! Oops! Come on! You must be kidding.

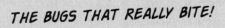

THE WORST OFFENDERS

THE BUGS THAT REALLY BITE!

*T*he "Worst Offenders" section includes an infestation of the errors that I see and hear most frequently, and that make me cringe or cry or sigh! These issues constantly show up on state exams and on college placement and job application tests. I put them here in the beginning of *The Bugaboo Review* because they lead the swarm of mistakes made by those who are unclear, and I want my students to learn them first. I encourage you to do the same.

accept/except

To accept is a verb meaning "to receive"; *except* is usually a preposition meaning "excluding." Examples: I will *accept* all the boxes *except* that one. Students gladly *accept* an A because they've earned it!

advice/advise

Advice is a noun, something you give or take (think of *vice* as a noun, a thing); *advise* is a verb. Examples: When you're wise, you may *advise*. We *advise* you to take John's *advice*.

affect/effect

To affect is a verb meaning "to influence" or "to put on a show of"; *effect* is usually a noun meaning "result" or "a changed state due to action by someone or something." Less often, *to effect* is used as a verb meaning "to bring about." Examples: The drug did not *affect* the disease, and it had several adverse side *effects*. The principal's plan *affected* the students and *effected* great change, which was its most positive *effect*. (Think: th*e effect*.)

among/between

Use *among* when referring to three or more people or things; use *between* for two items or people. Examples: You and Gregory discuss this *between* the two of you; Grant, Megan, and I will talk *among* ourselves.

anybody, anyone, anything
everybody, everyone, everything
somebody, someone, something
nobody, no one, nothing

This is the issue of pronoun agreement. All these terms are singular and take a singular verb and a singular pronoun. Examples: *Anybody* who *has* done *his* or *her* (not *their*) laundry may leave. *Has* **everybody** lost *his* or *her* (not *their*) mind? *Everyone* had *his* or *her* (not *their*) opinion. **Someone** drove *his* or *her* (not *their*) car into a ditch! (Note: If the wording seems bulky, make the subject plural: *All* those who *have* done *their* laundry... *People* who *have* lost *their* golf clubs... Or replace the troublesome pronoun with an article: *Someone* drove *a* car. *Everyone* had *an* opinion.)

"anyways," "anywheres," "nowheres"

These are not standard words; use *anyway*, *anywhere*, and *nowhere*.

as/like

As is often used as a conjunction that introduces a subordinate clause. *Like* is usually a preposition, but not a conjunction, and should be followed by a noun, pronoun, or noun phrase, as in: "She looks *like* a doll." In formal writing use them correctly: "You don't know her *as* I do" is correct; it is not correct to say, "You don't know her *like* I do." Or use *as if*: "He looks *as if* (not *like*) he hasn't slept in a week." Of course, *to like* also is a verb meaning "to take pleasure in" or "to find agreeable," as in: "I *like* lemon gelato!" (*Like* is NOT a fill-in word! See the discussion of *like* as a sentence filler in the Body of the Bug that follows.)

bad/badly

Bad is an adjective and describes a noun or pronoun; *badly* is an adverb, so it modifies a verb, an adjective, or another adverb. "I felt badly" indicates that your fingers didn't *function* well, as if they were frozen or numb, because *badly* describes the act of feeling, not you, the person (a pronoun or noun). Examples: I felt *bad* that Kendra had moved away. Yasmeen has done *badly* on her home project; paint is splattered everywhere! (Note: When in doubt, test your sentence by changing the word *badly* to another word, like *coldly* or *sadly*. You wouldn't say, "I felt coldly" or "I felt sadly"; these are incorrect and sound weird!)

bring/take

Use *bring* when an object is being transported toward you; use *take* when it is being moved away, as in: "Please *bring* me some water, then *take* these flowers to Mrs. Lan." (Think of "take-out" food, which you "take away.") There is a small exception, however. According to the *American Heritage Guide to Contemporary Usage and Style* (2005), "when the point of reference is not the place of speaking itself, either verb is possible, but the correct choice still depends on the desired perspective." So if you're speaking of an upcoming event that will take place elsewhere, you might say, "What may I **bring** to the party?" The event's host might reply, "You may **bring** dessert." (By the way, it's never *brang* or *brung*.)

conc**ei**ve, dec**ei**ve, perc**ei**ve, rec**ei**ve

(See "ei" and "ie" section on page 201.)

"could of," "may of," "might of," "must of," "should of," "would of"

Use the verb **have**, not the preposition *of*, after verbs such as **could**, **should**, **would**, **may**, **might**, and **must**. Examples: They **must have** (not *must of*) left. I **may have** (not *may of*) said that I would go with you.

de**finite**ly, inde**finite**ly

Fin and *finite* appear in both of these words; there are no *a*'s. (Note: Your computer spell-checker may change **definitely** to *defiantly*, so don't wing it by using your computer to supply the correct spelling!)

each, either

Each is singular; so is *either*. Examples: *Each* has (not *have*) *his* or *her* (not *their*) own idea. *Either* of the flavors *is* (not *are*) fine with me. (If you have trouble remembering this, add a mental *one*: *Each one* has his or her passion.)

fewer/less

Fewer refers to items that can be counted, *less* to general amounts. Examples: *Fewer* people live in the city, but they have *less* space there than in the country.

good/well

Good is an adjective and describes a noun or pronoun; *well* is an adverb and describes a verb, an adjective, or another adverb, as in: "He did a *good* job on the relay and came out *well* in the standings." *Good* (an adjective) describes the *job* (a thing, a noun); *well* (an adverb) describes *how* he *did* (a verb, which in this case shows action).

I or me — a trick to remember when using these so you don't get stung

"*Him and I* went," "*her and I* talked," "*me and Liz* did it," "*Juan and him* ate" — and any similar example of a compound subject: these are *incorrect*! To check yourself, mentally remove or block out one of the subjects and hear how the sentence sounds: "*him* went," "*her* talked," "*me* did it," "*him* ate." These obviously are wrong, so say instead, for example: *He and I* went (he went, and I went). *She and I* talked (she talked, and I talked). *Liz and I* like to dance (Liz likes to dance, and I like to dance). More examples when using I or me: "She read the map to Julio and *I*" or "...Julio and *me*"? Remove the words *Julio and*. Would you say: "She read the map to *me*" or "...to *I*"? *Me* is correct, not "Julio and *I*." Remember, when it's the subject of a sentence, always use *I*. Examples: Jo and *I* like to dance. Ben and *I* will go. He and *I* want to leave early.

its/it's

Its, which has no apostrophe, is a possessive pronoun showing that something owns something; *it's = it is*. The apostrophe in *it's* indicates that the letter *i* has been omitted; it is not an issue of possession in this case. Examples: *It's* time we washed our puppy; *its* little paws are muddy!

lay/lie

To lay is to place something or put something down, and it must be followed by a noun or pronoun, a thing; *to lie* is to recline. A *lie* is an untruth, and *to lie* also means "to tell an untruth." Examples: *Lay* that package on the mantel, will you please? Bridgette would like to *lie* in the hammock near the pool. Sometimes it's tempting to *lie* when you're in trouble, but a *lie* only makes things worse. (Hint: *Lay* sounds like p*la*ce; *lie* sounds like rec*lie*ne. But be careful: *lay* is also the past tense of the verb *to lie*: Jay *lay* on the couch all day yesterday.)

LIE

LAY

loose/lose

Loose is an adjective that means "not securely fastened"; *to lose* is the verb meaning "to misplace, to rid, or not to win." Examples: If you *lose* weight, your clothes may be t*oo* *loose*. (Hint: *lose* and *lost* come from the same root, and each has four letters.)

neither/none

Neither is singular, as in: "*Neither* (one) of the boys failed *his* test." *None*: I was taught that *none* is short for *not one*. But some contend that *none* usually is used with an amount that can't be counted, such as "none of it" — as in: "*None* of the milk *was* spilled" — and that if *none* refers to something that can be counted, then it takes a plural verb: "*None* of the eggs *are* broken." I still say, though, that *none* (not one) is singular, as in: "*None* (not one) of the eggs *is* broken." Also, the word *neither* is part of the "ei" and "ie" section at the end of the book.

passed/past

Passed is the past (!) tense of the verb *to pass*; *past*, an adjective or preposition, means "belonging to a former time" or "beyond a time or place." *Past* can also be a noun. Examples: Mom *passed* the pizza while our *past* president spoke. The hotel is just *past* the fountain. His *past* finally caught up with him.

possessive pronouns and apostrophes

Pronouns that show ownership, called "possessive pronouns," do not have apostrophes. Examples: *theirs, yours,*

ours, hers, his, its. This is odd because possessive *nouns* MUST have apostrophes: *Bob's,* the *dog's, children's, parent's, parents'.*

DOUBLE TROUBLE FROM THESE CREEPY CRAWLIES

These words have double letters:

a<u>cc</u>o<u>mm</u>odate	para<u>ll</u>el
a<u>cc</u>omplish	prefe<u>rr</u>ed
a<u>dd</u>r<u>ess</u>	qui<u>zz</u>es
a<u>pp</u>arently	reco<u>mm</u>end
a<u>pp</u>earance	roo<u>mm</u>ate
a<u>ss</u>a<u>ss</u>ination	ski<u>ll</u>ful
di<u>ss</u>atisfied	transfe<u>rr</u>ed
emba<u>rr</u>a<u>ss</u>	

These words are especially tricky:

co<u>mm</u>itment
co<u>mm</u>i<u>tt</u>ed
co<u>mm</u>i<u>tt</u>ee
refe<u>rr</u>al
refe<u>rr</u>ed
refe<u>r</u>ence (a single *r* – be careful)

separate

There's *a rat* in *sep**a**rate*. It's not spelled "sep**e**rate."

than/then

Than is a conjunction used in comparisons; *then* is an adverb denoting time. Examples: This is more *than* I can handle now; let's stop, *then* talk again tomorrow. Zane is taller *than* I am.

their/there/they're

Their is a possessive pronoun, as in: "It's *their* turn to pay." *There* is an adverb specifying place, or where something is located. (Hint: *Here* and *there* both speak of place, and the word *here* actually appears inside the word *there*. "Sylvia is lying *there*." *There* is also an interjection, something that shows feelings, as in: "*There*! Now look at what you've done!" *They're* is a contraction of *they are*, as in: "*They're* happy." (A contraction is a combination of words, with an apostrophe ['] in place of a missing letter or letters.) (See "ei" and "ie" section on page 201.)

there are/there's

Use *are* when the subject is plural; don't use "there's many." The subject and the verb must agree, as in: "*There are* many *people* who work." (Think: Many *people are* working.) It's not: "*There's* (there is) many people who work." Examples: *There's* a lot of *mud* on the road. (*Mud is* on the road.) *There is* much *work* to do. *There are* many *things* to do.

threw/through

Threw is the past tense of the verb **to throw**; **through** is a preposition, or an adverb meaning "in at one side, end, or surface — and out the other," or "to the end." Examples: Chad **threw** the ball **through** (preposition) the window! David will see the project **through** (adverb) to its brilliant conclusion.

to/too/two

To is a preposition (always followed by a noun or pronoun) meaning "a direction toward a point"; it's also part of the infinitive, or basic form, of a verb (such as **to sing**, **to dream**, **to play**, **to study**). *Too* is an adverb meaning "also or in addition" or "more than is desirable." (Think: The extra *o* is **too** many!) *Two* is the number after **one**. Examples: **To dance** (infinitive) is fun for **two to do**; for some, though, it is **too** strenuous, so they go **to** a movie instead.

who's/whose

Who's is the contraction of **who is**. (A contraction is a combination of words, with an apostrophe ['] in place of a missing letter or letters.) *Whose* is a pronoun, the possessive (showing ownership or possession) of **who** used as an adjective. Examples: **Who's** the one who said, "**Whose** umbrella did I take?"

your/you're

Your is a possessive pronoun; *you're* is a contraction of **you are**. (A contraction is a combination of words, with an apostrophe ['] in place of a missing letter or letters.) Examples: **You're** the one who is responsible for **your** actions.

THE ABSOLUTES — DON'T OVERDO IT!

Certain words are called "absolutes" and cannot have degrees attached to their use — use them without adverb modifiers (*most*, *very*, *quite*, and so on). Examples: my favorite, a unique outlook, the perfect sport, one final draft.

Don't use phrases such as *more unique*, *very favorite*, *most perfect*, *very final draft*, *very best*, *almost correct*, *fairly complete*. The following is a list of some of the absolutes:

best	first
complete	free
correct	last
dead	perfect
end	pregnant
equal	unique
excellent	worst
favorite	wrong
final	

THE BODY OF THE BUG

This is the main section of *The Bugaboo Review* — the "thorax," as my students suggest. Again, the issues I cover here relate primarily to formal writing and conversation, but also to decent dialogue among the well informed. The issues appear in alphabetical order. Words with tricky spellings stand alone, with the troublesome areas underlined and, in some cases, hints to help you remember them. Quotation marks around subheadings signify incorrect usage or spelling; the corrections follow them. Italicized subheadings denote items of interest that don't quite fit into a particular category. Items repeated from the "Worst Offenders" section are marked "W.O." Each of the items in the publication is included to help you navigate around the hornet's nest that is the English language!

absence
Hint: If you don't work out, you may have an *__absence__* of *abs* and other muscles.

accede/exceed
To accede is to give one's consent; *to exceed* is to extend beyond or be greater than. Examples: I *accede* to your staying out past curfew, but don't *exceed* your time limit; be home by midnight.

accept/except (W.O.)
To accept is a verb meaning "to receive"; *except* is usually a preposition meaning "excluding." Examples: I will *accept* all the packages *except* that one.

accident**ally**

Hint: Your *ally*, or partner, was in an accident [*accident-ally*], but she is finally doing better.

a**cc**o**mm**odate

Hint: *Accommodate* others by giving them two *c*'s and two *m*'s!

a**cc**omplish

a**cc**umulate

Hint: On your report card, you can *accumulate* two *c*'s, but not two *m*'s.

ach**ieve**ment

This is part of the "ei" and "ie" section beginning on p. 201, and there's an *Eve* in this word. Example: Isaiah has been given accolades for his great *ach**ieve**ment* of graduating.

acidic/ascetic/aesthetic

Acidic describes something "tending to form an acid, and tasting sharp or bitter," or "ill-tempered and sour." *Ascetic* means "austere, severe, unadorned, harsh"; *aesthetic* means "appealing to the senses — tasteful, pleasing, artistic." Examples: The old grump had an *acidic* temperament. Jennifer chose the plain, simple, *ascetic* life of a nun. Her lovely garden was pleasing and *aesthetic* to look at.

acknowledge
The words *know* and *ledge* are part of it: ac-know-ledge.

acknowledgment/judgment
Your choice: *acknowledgment/acknowledgement*, and *judgment/judgement* — include the extra *e* or not (the British do include the extra *e*).

acquaintance

acquire

across
Only one *c*. Hint: There is *a cross* on the church *across* the street.

addition/edition
Addition is the act of adding; for example, you add numbers to find a sum. It also is something added, such as an app or a room. *Edition* is the total number of copies of a publication, or a version of a show or publication. Examples: Students, do your *addition* problems for tomorrow. The *addition* of the patio created a beautiful yard. The morning *edition* of the *Times* had the same stories as did the evening *edition* of the six o'clock news.

address
Hint: You glance at the department store ad and there's a great dress featured; it's an *ad dress*!

adventure/venture
An *adventure* is an unusual experience or an undertaking or enterprise, often of a hazardous or exciting nature; a *venture* is similar, but it is an undertaking that is daring,

risky, or dangerous or has an uncertain outcome. Examples: Our trip to the little town of Gualala proved to be an *adventure* when the winding road above the bay was blocked by seven cows in no hurry to move! Richard's investment in solid gold windshield wipers proved to be a disastrous financial *venture*.

adverse/averse

Adverse means "unfavorable"; *averse* means "opposed to" or "reluctant"; *averse* is usually followed by *to*. Examples: I am *averse to* your idea; putting it into practice will have an *adverse* effect.

advice/advise (W.O.)

Advice is a noun, something you give or take (think of *vice* as a noun, a thing); *advise* is a verb. Examples: Anyone who is wise will *advise* you to take my *advice*!

affect/effect (W.O.)

To affect is a verb meaning "to influence," or "to put on a show of"; *effect* is usually a noun meaning "result" or "a changed state due to action by someone or something." Less often, *to effect* is used as a verb meaning "to bring about." Examples: Her trying to *affect* a phony accent did not *affect* Meg's reputation, but the *effect* was that it ruined some friendships. (Think: th<u>e</u> <u>e</u>ffect.) Only the Senate can *effect* a change such as that.

affinity/infinity

An *affinity* is a natural liking for, or an identification with, something or someone; *infinity* is endless distance, time, quantity. Examples: Her loving *affinity* for him will last into *infinity*.

affluent/effluent

Affluent is an adjective meaning "having an abundance of material wealth"; *effluent* is a noun meaning "liquid waste discharged from a sewage system or factory," or an adjective describing that waste, or a stream or river that flows from a larger body of water. Examples: The mansion of the *affluent* family was not near the *effluent*, bubbling sewage system.

afterward, afterwards

These are interchangeable, but *afterward* is preferred. Example: Let's go to the county fair and have corn dogs and cotton candy and funnel cake; *afterward* we can go on all the rides — if we're not ill by then!

aggravate/agitate/irritate

To aggravate means "to make worse or more troublesome," as in: "Overgrazing *aggravated* the erosion problem." In formal writing avoid the colloquial use of *aggravate* to mean "to annoy or bother," which is the definition of *irritate*. *To agitate* means "to make someone feel nervous or anxious," or "to stir up, as trouble." Examples: Her babbling *irritated* (not *aggravated*) me. Protestors began to *agitate* the crowd into a riot. The intense smoke from the barbeque *aggravated* my already itching eyes.

agree to/agree with

To agree to means "to give approval or consent to"; *to agree with* means "to be in accord with or to come to an understanding with." Examples: Nils *agrees with* me about the change, but he won't *agree to* my plan.

aid/aide/AIDS

To aid is to help or furnish with assistance; as a noun, *aid* is the act or result of helping. An *aide* is an assistant or helper; *AIDS* is a disease of the immune system. Examples: We will give *aid* to those who suffered in the tsunami. Julianna is a Peace Corps *aide* at the *AIDS* clinic in Malawi.

air/aire/err/ere

These all sound about the same, but *air* is a gaseous mixture that we breathe, or the sky, or a huge void, as in: "As we breathed the clean *air*, our troubles vanished into thin *air*." An *aire* (or *air*) is a tune or melody sung solo in an opera or oratorio. *To err* is to make a mistake or error, as in Alexander Pope's famous line: "*To err* is human; to forgive, divine." *Ere* is Old English; as a preposition it means "previous to," and as a conjunction it means "before," as in: "*Ere* I go, I will seek the king's advice."

alimentary/elementary

Alimentary relates to nourishment; *elementary* means "basic." Examples: At Lindberg *Elementary* School, we learned about the functioning of the *alimentary* canal.

all of <u>a</u> sudden

The term is not "all of <u>the</u> sudden." Example: We were walking along Fisherman's Wharf when, *all of a sudden*, Lulu blurted out: "I'm starving; let's have some fresh crab!"

allowed/aloud

Allowed means "have permission to do" something; *aloud* means "using an audible (loud enough to hear) speaking voice." Examples: To the entire class, Ms. Chiang said *aloud*: "You are *allowed* to have two cookies each."

all ready/already

All ready means "completely prepared" (all is ready); *already* means "previously." Examples: Lila was *all ready* to go to the play, but her friends had *already* left.

all right/"alright"

All right is written as two words; "alright" is nonstandard in formal writing, so don't use it. Example: Let's make sure Susanna is *all right* before we go to the lake.

"alls"

Alls is not a word. Don't say, "Alls I have are these two pennies."

all together/altogether

All together means everyone in a group acts collectively, or everyone's together; *altogether* means "entirely." Examples: We were elated that we were *all together* eating turkey for Thanksgiving but hadn't been *altogether* sure that it would happen. (Note: Try this trick to decide which term to use: see whether the sentence still makes sense if you separate the words by inserting other words. "Darius, Sophia, and Jan were *all together* in the sunroom playing Monopoly. *All* the kids, Darius, Sophia, and Jan, were *together* playing Monopoly in the sunroom." If your sentence still works, use *all together*.)

allude/elude

To allude is to use an indirect reference; *to elude* is to avoid, evade, or escape. Both are verbs. Examples: Alfredo often *alludes* to Anna's hiding and *eluding* him after they broke up. (Hint: *Elude*, *escape*, and *evade* all begin with **e**.)

allusion/illusion

An *allusion* is an indirect reference (see *allude*); an *illusion* is a misconception or false impression. Examples: Liang made the *allusion* of going to the Big Apple, and I knew she meant New York, not the fruit! The magician made us believe he had a rabbit in his hat, but it was only an *illusion*; the bunny wasn't really in there, and we were disappointed because we wanted to pet the furry little guy. (Hint: *Ill* has a negative connotation; *illusion* is somewhat negative, as if being tricked.)

NO EXTRA "WORM-LIKE" S's

Don't add an s at the ends of these words:

afterward	everywhere
all	forward
anyway	onward
anywhere	toward
backward	upward
downward	

a lot

Yes, this is two words. *Alot* IS NOT A WORD! Example: Sometimes people spell this as one word, but it's two; it happens *a lot*!

altar/alter

An *altar* is a ceremonial table at the front of a church, or a sacrificial platform; the verb *to alter* means "to change." Examples: A lovely chalice sat on the *altar* near the pulpit of the cathedral. Being in a peaceful place can *alter* one's mood. (Hint: If you stretch your imagination, a church steeple looks a little like a capital *A* — and an *altar* is found in a church.)

ALTAR (INSIDE)

alternate/alternative

The verb *to alternate* means "to occur in succession" or "to pass back and forth from one place or thing to another," as in: "The children *alternated* between their parents' homes each weekend." As an adjective, *alternate* means "following in turns, or in place of another": "The team used *alternate* pitchers throughout the season." *Alternative* may be used when referring to a substitute, but when you mean "happening in turns," use *alternate*. Examples: We chose an ***alternative*** route for the trips we took on ***alternate*** vacations.

alumna/alumni/alumnus

An ***alumna*** is a female graduate or former student of a school, college, or university; an ***alumnus*** is a male of the same category; ***alumni*** is the plural of ***alumnus*** (male), and ***alumnae*** is the plural of ***alumna*** — though more often the two plurals are combined in the word ***alumni***, as the alternative is ***alumnae/i***, which few are willing to use! Examples: I am an ***alumna*** of Chapman University; my classmates and I are ***alumni***.

a.m./p.m., A.M./P.M.

When you use these abbreviations to indicate the time, it's your choice whether you want to capitalize them. For example, you might write ***6 a.m.*** or ***11 P.M.*** Don't use the abbreviations as substitutes for the words *morning* and *evening*, however. Write: "I worked until late in the evening," not "late in the p.m." Remember not to use these abbreviations in formal writing.

amateur/immature

Amateur means "nonprofessional, inexperienced"; ***immature*** means "childish or undeveloped." Examples: An ***amateur*** production of *Annie* was staged by a local troupe. The toddlers babbled in their ***immature*** way.

among

There's no *u* in this word; it's not spelled "amoung." Example: Lynzie, Mike, and Teagan talked ***among*** themselves about what to do on spring break.

among/between/amid (W.O.)

Use *among* when talking about three or more individuals or things; use *between* when referring to two; use *amid* when referring to a quantity of something that isn't made up of individual articles (use with *clouds*, *rain*, *forest*, and so on). Examples: The prize was divided *among* ten contestants. We tore our ticket in half and divided it *between* the two losers! They disappeared *amid* the shrubbery.

amoral/immoral

Amoral means "unconcerned about good behavior or morals," or "not concerned with moral judgments"; *immoral* means "morally wrong." Examples: Aunt Mo was *amoral*; she didn't judge others by their morals; however, she did feel that capital punishment was *immoral*.

amount/number

Use *amount* with quantities that cannot be counted; use *number* with those that can. Examples: It is a huge *amount* of dough; no wonder...it uses a large *number* of cups of flour — ten! (Hint: You can't count an *amount*!)

amuse/bemuse

To amuse is to hold someone's attention or interest in a pleasant way; *to bemuse* means "to confuse or bewilder, to befuddle." As an adjective, *bemused* means "lost in thought or preoccupied." Examples: We were *amused* watching the comedian who acted *bemused* and bewildered; it was his act!

anal_yze_

anc_ie_nt

This word is part of the "ei" and "ie" section beginning on p. 201. Example: The glorious, **ancient** hills of Rome have seen centuries of history.

"and etc.," "and/or," "and so"

Don't use these in formal writing — and whether you're writing or speaking, "*and etc.*" is never correct.

"angry at," angry with

You're not *angry at* someone; you're **angry with** him or her because you're both human and relate *with* each other.

angry/mad

To be **angry** is to feel resentment, outrage, or anger. **Mad**, while often interchanged with the word **angry**, actually means "suffering a disorder of the mind," "insane," or "deranged"; it's also used to mark confusion or excitement, as in: "There was a **mad** scramble to get tickets." Or it can be used to show strong liking for something: "Kimmie was **mad** about the new musical!"

annals/annul

Annals are yearly records; **to annul** means "to make something invalid or void." Examples: The town's **annals** showed that only seven couples had filed **to annul** their marriages.

annual/ biannual/semiannual/ biennial/perennial

Annual events happen once every year; **biannual** or **semi-annual** events occur twice a year; **biennial** events happen every two years. To distinguish **biannual** from **biennial**, remember the **-ennial** suffix means "every certain number of years," as in the dec**ennial** census (every ten years) and the United States bicent**ennial** in 1976. **Perennial** means "lasting or active through the year or through many years." Example: **Perennial** plants, such as daffodils, bloom every year, and sometimes throughout the year.

ante/anti

The prefix **ante** means "earlier" or "in front of"; the prefix **anti** means "opposed to" or "against." Examples: Northerners supported the **anti**slavery movement during the **ante**bellum period. (Note: **Anti** should be used with a hyphen when it is followed by a capital letter or a word beginning with *i*: **anti**-Nazi, **anti**-inflammation, **anti**-American.)

anxious/eager, anxiously/eagerly

Anxious means "worried about or apprehensive." Avoid using **anxious** to mean "eager." Examples: We are **eager** (not *anxious*) to see your new puppy. I'm **anxious** about Friday's final exams. I **eagerly** await his return.

anybody, anyone, anything
everybody, everyone, everything
somebody, someone, something
nobody, no one, nothing (W.O.)

This is the issue of pronoun agreement. All these terms are singular and take a singlular verb and a singular pronoun. Examples: **Anybody** who **has** taken **his** or **her** (not *their*) gift may go. Did **anyone** leave **his** (not *their*) tie here? **Has everybody** eaten **his** or **her** (not *their*) pizza?

Somebody has left **his** or **her** (not *their*) books. **Everyone** had **his** or **her** (not *their*) opinion. **Someone** drove **his** or **her** (not *their*) car into a ditch! If the wording seems bulky, make the subject plural: "**All those** who have claimed their gifts…**People** who have lost their way…The **children** have gotten their pizza." Or use an article instead of a pronoun: "**Somebody** has left **a** tie. Has **everyone** brought **a** pie?"

anymore

Use the adverb **anymore** to mean "any longer," as in: "Moviegoers are rarely shocked **anymore** by profanity." Use **now** or **nowadays** instead. Example: Cars are so expensive **nowadays** (not *anymore*) that many people are biking. (Note: **Anymore** cannot be used as an adjective or an adverb modifying another adjective or another adverb. It is incorrect to say: "There isn't *anymore* popcorn" or "I couldn't have eaten *anymore* slowly." Use the two words **any more**.)

anyone/any one

Anyone is an indefinite pronoun and means "any person at all." In the term **any one**, the pronoun **one**, which is preceded by the adjective **any**, refers to a particular person or thing in a group. Examples: Has **anyone** seen my tennis ball? You may choose **any one** of the plants to take with you.

"anyplace"

Anyplace is an informal term for **anywhere**; avoid using it in formal writing.

TRICKY SPELLINGS

amat<u>eur</u>   rh<u>y</u>thm

man<u>eu</u>ver   <u>s</u>ergeant

play<u>wr</u>ight   solilo<u>quy</u>

pre<u>j</u>udice   su<u>b</u>tly

priv<u>ilege</u>   vac<u>uu</u>m

"anyways," "anywheres," "nowheres" (W.O.)

Anyways, *anywheres*, and *nowheres* are not standard words. None of these terms takes an *s*. Instead, write: *anyway*, *anywhere*, and **nowhere**.

a part/apart

A part means "a portion of"; **apart** means "separated," "distanced," or "special." Examples: **A part** of me cares for Max, but not enough to marry him. **Apart** from the distance and the winding coastal road, the drive to Mendocino is enticing; and the town is charming.

ap<u>p</u>arently

Remember the two **p**'s — and that the word **parent** is in it.

ap<u>pear</u>ance

There's a **pear** in ap**pear**ance...then <u>ance</u>.

apposite/opposite

Apposite means "especially well suited to the circumstances"; *opposite* means "facing a different direction," or "somebody or something totally different from another." Examples: The sunshine was *apposite* for the outdoor wedding. Your opinion is the *opposite* of mine; we totally disagree.

appraise/apprise

To appraise is to evaluate or size up; *to apprise* is to inform. Examples: He *apprised* me that the painting was *appraised* at millions!

appropriate

Notice the two *p*'s in the first syllable. Hint: "I <u>appro</u>ve of your being *<u>appro</u>priate*."

arbiter/arbitrary

An *arbiter* is a judge; *arbitrary* means "based on a whim," or "based on personal wishes or feelings, rather than facts." Examples: The *arbiter* in the case of the missing fudge was Grandpa. It was an *arbitrary* and capricious decision.

ar<u>c</u>tic

Hint: There's an *arc* in *<u>arc</u>tic*

are/our

Are is a verb form of *to be*; *our* is a possessive pronoun. Examples: They *are our* ideas.

argument

Hint: *Gum* is in the word, but there's no *argument* about it: no gum is allowed in school!

argumentative

It's not spelled "argumentive." Add the extra *ta*.

aroma/fragrance/odor

An *aroma* is a pleasant smell; a *fragrance* is a sweet and pleasant odor, or a substance (like perfume or cologne); an *odor* is a smell or scent, whether pleasant or unpleasant. Examples: The *aroma* of my Aunt Katie's strudel wafted through the house. The *fragrance* of Raymond's aftershave lotion leaves a pleasant memory — a nice *odor* to remind her of his presence.

arrant/errant

Arrant means "outrageously so or extreme"; *errant* means "wandering." Examples: Jacob's *errant* mind would not focus on the subject at hand. Marcie's *arrant* behavior landed her in the principal's office.

as/because/since

These terms can be ambiguous and confusing; the word *as* is sometimes used to mean "because," but do not use it if there is any chance of ambiguity (double meaning), as in: "We canceled the picnic *because* (not *as*) it began raining." *As* here could mean either "because" or "when," so it would be unclear if used. Generally, use *as* to denote time, as in: "*As* I was jogging, I saw a fawn." Use *because* in relation to reason or cause, as in: "**Because** I am older than you, I should go first."

as/like (W.O.)

As is often used as a conjunction that introduces a sub-ordinate clause — for example: "**As** it was warm yesterday, Cooper didn't take a sweater today." **Like** is usually a preposition, but not a conjunction, and should be followed by a noun or pronoun: "Lee looks **like** Mom." In formal writing use them correctly: "Victor doesn't know her **as** I do" is correct; it is not correct to say, "You don't know her *like* I do." Or use **as if**: Arturo looks **as if** (not *like*) he hasn't slept in a week. **To like** is a verb meaning "to take pleasure in" or "to find agreeable," as in: "I **like** lemon gelato!" (**Like** is *not* a sentence filler! See the discussion of "like" below.)

ascent/assent

An **ascent** is an upward climb. An **assent** is an agreement. **To assent** is the same as the verb **to agree**. Examples: I **assent** to your claim that it's difficult to make an **ascent** up Mount Whitney. (Hint: Both as**c**ent and **c**limb have **c**'s.)

a<u>sk</u>

The pronunciation is "ask," not "aks" or "ast." The mispronunciations come from certain dialects of parts of the United States, and from Old English and Middle English. (Variant pronunciations are evident in, for example, Chaucer's book *Canterbury Tales*, which was written in Middle English.) As President Kennedy implored, "**Ask** not what your country can do for you; **ask** what you can do for your country."

aspire/inspire

To aspire is to seek to attain a specific goal; **to inspire** is to encourage greater efforts, or more enthusiasm and creativity, in another person. "I **aspire** to do my best, and my life teachers **inspire** me to do so."

assassination

Hint: There are two donkeys — that is, two **asses** — in **assassination**!

assess

This word, which means "to judge or evaluate something," has two sets of **s**'s.

assure/ensure/insure

Each of these words means "to make sure or certain," but **assure** refers to making a **person** feel at ease; **insure** has come to refer to a guarantee against risk, as with an insurance policy; and **ensure** generally means "to make sure." Examples: Can you **assure** me that this policy will **insure** my car with enough coverage to **ensure** that my new Maserati's dents will be repaired?

asterisk

This is the term for the sign *. It is an **asterisk**, so don't pronounce it "asterick." It is used to call attention to something in a printed work.

astigmatism/stigmatism/stigma

An *astigmatism* or *stigmatism* is a visual defect that results in blurred vision. A *stigma* is the condition of having a unique birthmark or scar, or a mark of infamy or disgrace. Examples: Dana's *astigmatism* was corrected with the proper lenses. The thief was recognized by the *stigma* on his face — the heart-shaped birthmark, ironically, gave away his identity.

atheism, atheist, atheistical, atheistically

An *atheist* is a person who denies the existence of God or gods. (See "ei" and "ie" section on page 201.)

athlete

When saying or spelling the word, remember that it has two syllables, not three — *ath-lete* (not *ath-a-lete*). Same with *athletics*.

attendance

It's spelled *attendance*; think of "attend the *dance*."

"at this point in time"

This is redundant and lengthy — just say "*at this time*" or "*now*."

audience

It's spelled *ience*, and it is part of the "ei" and "ie" section beginning on page 201.

aural/oral

Aural pertains to hearing or the ears, while **oral** pertains to the mouth or to speaking, singing, humming, and so forth.

avenge/revenge

Avenge is a verb meaning "to inflict punishment on someone for wrongdoing"; *revenge* as a noun refers to retaliation, to what is done to get even for a wrongdoing. As a verb, *revenge* is similar to *avenge* and means "to get even with someone." Examples: I will **avenge** the crushing of my petunias by getting *revenge* on the one who stomped on them!

avocation/vocation

An *avocation* is something one does as a hobby or pastime, rather than as a full-time job; a *vocation* is a job or career. Examples: Janet's *vocation* was teaching chemistry, but her *avocation* was performing magic tricks for children's parties; she enjoyed doing that.

aweigh

The phrase is "anchors **aweigh**," not "anchors *away*," when ships are about to set sail. It's a nautical term that has to do with the anchor's clearing the sea bottom beneath the vessel so it can move, and it means "to weigh anchor." (See "ei" and "ie" section on page 201.)

awful

Only one *l* — just as in *beautiful, wonderful, hopeful, painful, dutiful, grateful,* and so on. The word means "terrible" or "extremely bad"; don't use it in place of **very**. Example:

The bumpy ride with the flat tire was *awful*. (Don't say, "The trip was awful bad.")

a while/awhile

The two-word form *a while* is a noun preceded by an article and can be the object of a preposition, as in: "Stay for *a while*." *Awhile* is an adverb; it can modify a verb ("stay *awhile*") but cannot be the object of a preposition, such as *for* (do not say, "for *awhile*").

awkward

The spelling of this word is, well, *awkward*.

bachelor

No *t* in this word. (It's not "ba<u>t</u>chelor.")

backward/backwards

The words *backward* and *backwards* are interchangeable, but *backward* is preferred. As an adjective, it modifies a noun or pronoun, as in: "Angela gave a *backward* glance at the old house." As an adverb, *backward* modifies a verb, an adjective, or another adverb, as in" "Jorge looked *backward* to his life in the sixties." *Backward* is also a slang word, a negative term describing someone or something not very cultured or trendy. Example: That geek is socially pretty *backward*.

bad/badly (W.O.)

Bad is an adjective and describes a noun or pronoun; *badly* is an adverb, so it modifies a verb, an adjective, or another adverb. If you say, "Jessica felt badly," it means that her fingers didn't work well. This is because *badly* describes the act of feeling, not Jessica, the person (a pronoun or noun). When in doubt, test your sentence by changing the word **badly** to another word, such as **sad**. You wouldn't say, "Marc felt sadly"; that would be incorrect.

baited/bated

Baited is the past tense of the verb **to bait**, meaning "to set a trap" or "to entice"; **bated** means "moderated or restrained." So, regarding that old saying: we wait with **bated** breath, not *baited*.

barely/barley

Be careful not to misplace the **e** in these words. **Barely** means "hardly or scarcely"; **barley** is a grain.

baring/bearing/barring

Baring, pronounced "bairing," is an act of uncovering or revealing, or exposing, as in: "Step away; the dog is **baring** his teeth." **Bearing**, same pronunciation, has several meanings as a verb: "carrying or supporting" ("Carmen is **bearing** a grudge"); "having a tolerance for or enduring" ("**Bearing** his lies is something that Zeng can no longer do"); "producing or yielding" ("That little bush has been **bearing** gardenias all summer!"). Finally, it means "proceeding in a specified direction," as in: "This man-made path has been **bearing** toward the sea for nearly a mile." As a noun, a **bearing** is a device that supports or reduces friction between moving parts, as in a **bearing wall** or a **ball bearing**; it's also an awareness of one's position or surroundings, as in: "Katrina lost her **bearings** on the verdant road to lovely Calistoga." **Barring** means "excepting or aside from" or "fastening with a heavy bar": "**Barring** any more rain, we'll have a picnic on the church lawn. We'll be **barring** the gate at midnight."

bass

One type of **bass** (sounds like "mass") is a fish, either freshwater or sea **bass**. The other **bass** — same spelling, but pronounced "base" — refers to the lower register of the male voice or of musical instruments, as in "**bass** guitar."

bathos/pathos

Bathos (pronounced "bath'-os") refers to a sudden switch from the lofty and exalted to the commonplace, an anticlimax; **pathos** (pronounced "pay'-thos") is the quality of bringing forth feelings of compassion, sympathy, or pity. Examples: When world leaders are guilty of crimes and removed from their posts — one way or another — they experience **bathos**, and there are few of them who can evoke **pathos** from the public.

battery

A **battery** is an item that uses cells to produce electrical current; it's also a grouping of similar things used as a whole. In the military, a **battery** is the storage area for one or more pieces of artillery, or it is an artillery unit. **Battery** is also the act of pounding or beating. Examples: This computer takes four size C **batteries**. Janell took a **battery** of tests to discover her career path. The army kept the mortars and tanks in the **battery** near the canal. The suspects were booked on assault and **battery** charges.

bazaar/bizarre

A *bazaar* is a foreign marketplace or, originally, a sale to raise money for charity; *bizarre* means "amusingly grotesque, strange, or unusual." Examples: Rachael and I found a *bizarre* old mask at the annual church *bazaar*.

beck and call

The term is *beck and call* — not "*beckon call*"; it means "ready and willing to carry out a request." Example: I'm at your *beck and call*; just tell me what you need!

beginning

There are two *n*'s in the second syllable. Don't spell it "beggining"; the word is *begin*, with *ning* added.

ONE IS THE LONELIEST NUMBER

Use a singular verb with the following terms (to check yourself, try adding an imaginary one *or a version of it after some of the words, and mentally listen to how the sentence sounds):*

each (one)
either (one)
neither (one)
none (not one)
anybody (any single body)
anyone (any one person)
everybody (every single body)
everyone (every single one)

b<u>ei</u>ge

Beige is a very light brown color. (See "ei" and "ie" section on page 201.)

be<u>in</u>g

(See "ei" and "ie" section on page 201.)

"being as how, being that"

Nonstandard. Don't use them; use *because* instead. Example: *Because* I awoke early (not *Being that* or *being as how*), I was able to see the sunrise.

bel<u>ie</u>f, bel<u>ie</u>ve

(See "ei" and "ie" section on page 201.)

bene<u>fit</u>ed

It seems as if this word should have two *t*'s — but it doesn't.

berth/birth

Berth is a space or compartment; *birth* is the process of being born. Examples: The ship had a *berth* in Long Beach. Sara gave *birth* to twins last June. (Think: <u>I</u> have a b<u>i</u>rthday.)

beside/besides

Beside means "at the side of or next to," as in: "The spy slept with a gun *beside* her bed." As a preposition *besides* means "except," as in: "Nobody *besides* Erin can have that pie." *Besides* is also an adverb meaning "moreover" or "also": "I'm full; *besides*, I don't like Brussels sprouts."

Boer/boor

The word *Boer* relates to the Dutch colonists in South Africa. A *boor* is a person who has bad manners, or who is rude and has little sense of decorum. Examples: When you go to South Africa, don't call someone a *boor*, or you may be misunderstood and a *Boer* descendant may be offended!

"boughten"

This is not a word; the word is *bought*. Example: I should have *bought* (not *boughten*) those shoes while they were on sale.

bouillon/bullion

Bouillon is a clear, seasoned chicken, beef, or vegetable broth, sometimes made from dehydrated cubes or stock; *bullion* is gold or silver considered as a mass — as ingots or bars — rather than by a value. (Hint: Think of _**bull**ion_ as a golden *bull*.)

brake/break

A *brake* is the device that stops a vehicle; *to break* is to separate or destroy; and the noun *break* is a timed stoppage, as in "take a *break*." Examples: You could *break* your bones if the *brakes* on your car or bike don't work!

BRAKE   BREAK

brava, bravo, bravi

It's time for a short Italian lesson and some cultural information: When honoring a female soloist or other individual, say to her: "*Brava*!" When a male soloist or other individual is being given accolades, the word is *bravo*; when two or more are being cheered, it's *bravi*. Of course, if the performance is extremely good, you might augment your praise and use: *bravissima*, *bravissimo*, or *bravissimi*.

breath/breathe/breadth

Breath is the noun; *to breathe* is the verb, the action of breathing. *Breadth* refers to the measure of something from side to side. Examples: Take a deep *breath*. It's important to *breathe*!

brilliant

Two *i*'s and two *l*'s — and there's an *ant* in it.

bring/take (W.O.)

Use *bring* when an object is being transported toward you; use *take* when it is being moved away, as in: "Please *bring* me a paper plate and plastic wrap, then *take* these cookies to school." But the correct word choice also can depend on perspective, on whether you are at the location you speak of. So if you're speaking of an upcoming event that will take place elsewhere, you might say, "What may I *bring* to the picnic?" The event's host might reply, "You may *bring* ice. (By the way, it's never *brung* or *brang*.)

broach/brooch

To broach is a verb meaning "to bring up for discussion or to put forth for consideration." *Brooch*, which refers to a large decorative pin, is pronounced the same way. Examples: Did you or Dad **broach** the subject of getting a car? This cameo **brooch** was a gift from my grandmother.

bruise

Strange spelling; beware of the silent *i*.

bunch

The term **bunch** is used to describe grapes, bananas, and other foods in a cluster; avoid using this word in reference to a gathering of people and other living things.

buried

It still sounds like **berried**, however. **Buried** describes something that has been put in a place and covered. Example: Mutsie **buried** her bone in the back yard; now she wants to chew on that muddy thing!

burst

To burst is a verb meaning "to come open or apart suddenly and violently"; *busted*, *bust*, and *bursted* are nonstandard past tenses of the verb and shouldn't be used; the correct one is **burst**. Example: The dam **burst** because of all the rain.

business

Sounds like it should be spelled "bisness," but the word *sin* is in it.

caffeine

Caffeine is a stimulant found in coffee, tea, and chocolate. (See "ei" and "ie" section on page 201.)

calendar/colander

A *calendar* is a device or system that calculates the days and months of the year; a *colander* is a bowl-shaped dish or pan with holes in it used for draining (usually) food.

Calvary/cavalry

In the Bible story, *Calvary* is the name of the hill outside Jerusalem on which Jesus was crucified; a *calvary* is an experience of great suffering. *Cavalry* is the part of the army trained to fight on horseback.

camaraderie

Don't forget that the first three vowels are all *a*'s. The word means "close friendship or a brotherly connection" and is related to the term *comrade*, but the spelling is different.

cannon/canon

A *cannon* is a large, mounted gun that fires heavy objects through a tubelike structure. A *canon* is a code of law, a principle, or a standard, and is also a term for certain music and for a specific employed member of a clergy or church.

"can't hardly," "can't scarcely," "can't barely"

These double negatives are incorrect uses of *can hardly*, *can scarcely*, and *can barely*. The correct use? Examples: Liliana *can hardly* wait for the parade. I *can scarcely* believe how much Catalina and Alexandra have grown!

canvas/canvass

Canvas is a heavy cloth used for sails or in painting; *to canvass* means "to survey or consult various people as to their opinions." Examples: The yacht's *canvas* sails shimmered on the sapphire sea. Hannah painted the landscape on **canvas**. We **canvassed** the club's members to see which plan they preferred.

capital/capitol

Capital refers to a city, or to wealth or resources; *capitol* refers to a building where lawmakers meet. Examples: In the **capitol** building in Sacramento, California's state **capital**, lawmakers met to discuss raising **capital** for their new programs. (One of my students offered this hint: You don't have to pay a <u>toll</u> to get into the **cap<u>i</u>tol** building — this helps you to remember the *o*.)

caricature/character

A **caricature** is a comic representation, usually a drawing, that emphasizes someone's distinct physical features; **character** is the set of qualities that make one distinct, or it is somebody unusual, or somebody in a book, movie, or theater production. Examples: **Caricatures** of Bob Hope and Richard Nixon portrayed each with a very long nose. The **characters** in the novel were learning magic.

carriage

Don't forget the *i* — same as in **marriage**. Examples: After their extraordinary wedding and personal marriage vows, the royal couple left the cathedral in a gilded **carriage**.

carrot/karat

The word **carrot** refers to the thin, orange, pointy root vegetable; a **karat** is a unit of measurement of precious metals or stones. Examples: **Carrots** are healthful to eat. Kathleen's spectacular six-**karat** ring was gorgeous!

KARAT

CARROT

cataract

This word has several meanings. It can refer to a disease of the eye in which a film covers the lens, and also to a large or high waterfall, or a deluge.

caught/cough

The vowel sounds in these words are the same, but be careful of the spelling — *caught* is the past tense of c*a*tch (with an *a*), and *to cough* is to expel air from the lungs loudly, or the noise that makes. Examples: Oh, dear; I'm afraid I *caught* Jeremy's cold, and now I *cough* all the time.

-cede *words*

The following words end in *cede*:

accede — to consent, often at someone's insistence; to move into a position of honor. Example: She will *accede* to the presidency.

antecede — to come before something.

concede — to yield or grant; to acknowledge.

intercede — to act as a mediator; to plead for another.

precede — to exist prior to something; to be in front.

recede — to move back from a point; to fade away.

secede — to withdraw formally from a group, organization, or alliance.

cede — to give up possession of; to relinquish.

Note that **supersede**, meaning "to take the place of," is spelled with an **s**.

-ceed *words*

These words end in *ceed*:

exceed — to go beyond or outside of.

proceed — to go forward; to move on in an orderly manner.

succeed — to accomplish something desired; to come after as heir or successor.

cemetery

No *a* in it — only *e* vowels. Hint: Eventually one gets into the *cemetery* with ease — with *eee*'s. It's okay to groan at the pun!

censor/censure/sensor

To censor is to remove or suppress material considered objectionable; *to censure* means "to criticize severely." A *sensor* is a device sensitive to light, temperature, radiation level, or the like, that transmits a signal to a measuring device. Examples: Schools' *censoring* of certain books has been *censured* by most people who oppose the practice.

census/consensus

Remember that *census* has two *s*'s, and *consensus* has three *s*'s. A *census* is an official periodic counting of people and a recording of demographic information; *consensus* means "a general or widespread agreement among a group." Examples: In the United states, a *census* to count the population is taken every ten years. There is a general *consensus* of opinion that Shea lives the good life in Rio!

changeable

Don't forget the first *e* — the word contains *change* + *able*.

changing

This one has no *e* — it's a *change* from the preceding term!

chord/cord

A *chord* is the combination of two or more tones sounded at the same time; a *cord* is a rope or string, or an insulated

CHORD

CORD

BOO

electric wire fitted with a plug to use as a conduit. Examples: The dissonant **chord** sung by the choir sounded like a cat screeching! The computer lab has a mass of **cords** crawling from the computers to the walls.

cicada/circadian

A *cicada* is an insect; *circadian* is an adjective that refers to a twenty-four-hour period, mainly in relation to biology (circadian rhythm). Examples: The shrill melody of the *cicadas* punctuated the evening's calm; the creatures were in *circadian* rhythm — harmonizing with nature as they played their dissonant tune every night, at twenty-four-hour intervals.

cite/sight/site

To cite means "to quote as an authority or example"; *sight* is the noun or object of seeing; *site* is usually a noun meaning "a particular place." Examples: Brandon **cited** the health code in his argument against the new **site** of the nuclear plant, which would block his **sight** of the picturesque hills.

clench/clinch

To clench is to close tightly, as with a clenched fist or clenched teeth; *to clinch* is to secure or settle definitely. Examples: After many instances of **clenched** teeth and groans of "Torture!" the San Francisco Giants **clinched** the National League pennant and then won the World Series!

climactic/climatic

Climactic is derived from **climax**, the point of greatest intensity in a series or progression of events; *climatic* refers to climate and meteorological conditions. Examples: The **climatic** condition of excessive rainfall caused immense flooding, the **climactic** and catastrophic event being the bursting of the levee.

clothes/cloths

The items you wear have an *e*; the **cloths** that **clothes** are made from do not. Examples: I like the choice of **clothes** Lucia wears. Many colored **cloths** were available in the bazaar.

coarse/course

Coarse means "rough in texture or crude"; **course** usually refers to a path, a playing field, or a unit of study. The term **of course** means "as is to be expected." Examples: The surface of the golf **course** was **coarse** due to the hail. Of **course**; I knew that! Jeb's language was **coarse**, so it was unpleasant to be around him.

codeine

Codeine is an alkaloid chiefly used to inhibit coughing. Example: Many over-the-counter cough medicines contain **codeine**. (See "ei" and "ie" section on page 201.)

collaborate/corroborate

To collaborate (co-_lab_or) is to work together to find a solution. (Hint: People in a **_lab_** work together.) **To corroborate** is to support with evidence, to confirm. Examples: Let's **collaborate** on the case to find someone who will **corroborate** his alibi and free him.

collage/college

A *collage* is an assemblage, such as a *collage* of memories. A *college* is an institution of higher learning that grants a bachelor's degree, or it is the undergraduate division of a university. Examples: I made a *collage* of my Europe trip souvenirs to hang on the wall of my dorm room at *college*.

colonel/colonial

A *colonel* is an officer in the U.S. Army, Air Force, or Marine Corps. The word sounds like *kernel*, but it's spelled *colonel*. (By the way, a *kernel* is a small seed or portion of something, as in "a *kernel* of corn.") *Colonial* relates to the original thirteen colonies that later became the United States, and to a style of furniture, art, or architecture of that period. Example: Scarlett's home was a *colonial* mansion, complete with a verandah and tall, white columns in the front.

colum<u>n</u>

Don't forget the *n* at the end. A *column* is a supporting pillar, with a base, a cylindrical, vertical shaft, and a top; it's also a formation of people (usually military) and vehicles, all following one behind another. In printing it's a vertical arrangement of typed lines that is set alongside others on a page. Examples: I read a *column* in the newspaper that said Company Q from the ROTC marched in a *column* in front of the *columned* capitol building.

co<u>m</u>ing

One *m*; it is *not* spelled "co<u>mm</u>ing." Example: Are you *coming* to my party tonight, Ariana?

commitment/committed/committee

Note the number of *m*'s and *t*'s.

compare to/compare with

Compare to is used when two unlike things are compared; use *compare with* when the comparison is between two similar things, which can either be compared or contrasted. Examples: "Shall I *compare* thee *to* a summer's day...?" Canned vegetables cannot *compare with* fresh ones from the garden; they just don't taste the same.

competitive

Derived from the same root as *competition*. Example: Athletes like Rob must constantly be *competitive* as they meet the grueling challenges of competition.

complacent/complicit

Complacent means "overly contented and unconcerned" or "eager to please"; *complicit* means "associated with or involved in a questionable act or a crime." Examples: We can be *complicit* in social crimes if we become *complacent* and do nothing to change inequitable situations.

complement/compliment

To complement is a verb meaning "to go with or complete"; *complement* is a noun referring to something that completes (these words have all *e* vowels). *To compliment* is a verb meaning "to flatter"; as a noun, a *compliment* is a flattering remark. (Hint: *I* like *compliments*!) Examples: Patty's painting ability *complements* her skill at decorating; she gets *compliments* on both.

comprise/compose

Comprise means "to consist of"; *compose* means "to make by combining" or "to put in proper form." Examples: The class *comprised* geniuses, each of whom could *compose* music.

concave/convex

Concave refers to a surface that's curved inward (think of "caved in"); *convex* means "having a surface that bulges outward or upward," as in the exterior of a sphere. Examples: The top of the cookie dough ice cream was *concave* after we'd finished scooping what we wanted from the container. After we piled the ice cream into dishes, the concoction in each was a *convex* dome just waiting for the hot fudge to be drizzled on it!

conceded/conceited

Conceded is the past tense of the verb *to concede*, which means "to acknowledge, often reluctantly, as the truth, or to admit." *Conceited* means "having a favorable and exaggerated image of one's own importance." Examples: Councilman Jones has *conceded* defeat in the election; people voted against him because he was so hubristic and *conceited*. (See "ei" and "ie" section on page 201.)

conceivable

No *e* after the *v*. *Conceivable* describes something that can be believed, understood, or mentally developed. Examples: It is *conceivable* that Joshua has taken a different route and that's why he isn't here yet; it's *inconceivable* that he merely left late. (See "ei" and "ie" section on page 201.)

conceive (W.O.)

The verb **to conceive** means "to imagine, to form a notion, or to become pregnant with." Examples: I can't **conceive** the idea that people think it's acceptable to unwrap food and to talk during theater performances; it's simply rude. It's difficult to **conceive** of the concept of infinite space. (See "ei" and "ie" section on page 201.)

conducive/conductive

Conducive means "tending to promote or assist"; **conductive** refers to having properties of conductivity. Examples: Attending college is **conducive** to your getting a good job. Metal is **conductive** in that it can attract lightning.

congratulations

The letter in the middle is a **t** not a **d**. The word is not "congradulations." Hint: Think of **congrats**.

conscience/conscious

Conscience is a noun meaning "scruples or moral principles"; **conscious** is an adjective meaning "aware or alert." Examples: Let your **conscience** be your guide; are you **conscious** that you should do that? (See "ei" and "ie" section on page 201.)

conscientious

Part of this word is also found in the word <u>scien</u>ce, so that may help you to remember it. **Conscientious** means "meticulous and careful about what you're doing." (See "ei" and "ie" section on page 201.)

consummate

This word has different meanings, with different pronunciations: The adjective, pronounced "con'-sum-mit," means "perfect, skilled, or complete in every way," as in: "Mozart was the consummate musician." The verb *to consummate*, pronounced "con'-sum-mayt," means "to bring to completion, finalize, or fulfill," often in reference to — ahem — what allegedly happens on the honeymoon night!

contemptible/contemptuous

Contemptible means "despicable and deserving to be treated with contempt"; *contemptuous* means "feeling strong dislike or lack of respect for somebody or something." Examples: Because the sci-fi monster in the movie was *contemptible*, all the gremlins in the village were *contemptuous* of him and wanted him to leave.

continence/continents

The word *continence* means "self-restraint and moderation"; it also refers to voluntary control over certain bodily functions, as well as abstention from sexual activity. *Continents* are the principal landmasses of the earth. Example: The world-class boxer practiced rigorous *continence* prior to a championship fight, and it worked: he was the most acclaimed boxer on all seven *continents*.

contingency/contingent

A *contingency* is an event that might occur in the future, such as a problem, emergency, or expense. *Contingent* as an adjective means "dependent on what may happen in the future"; as a noun it denotes a group of people representing a belief, or an organization. Examples: Let's devise a **contingency** plan in case it rains on picnic day. Their plans were **contingent** upon whether their money held out! The Illinois **contingent** entered the convention hall.

continual/continuous

Continual means "repeated regularly and often"; *continuous* means "extended or prolonged without interruption." Examples: Julia hated the **continual** negative political ads. The alarm bell was jammed and rang **continuously**; it never stopped and was making Gayle loony!

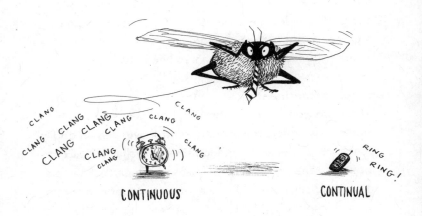

CONTINUOUS   CONTINUAL

convenient

Remember that **ven** is the tricky part. **Convenient** means "fitting one's comfort, purpose, or needs." Example: It was **convenient** that there was a *convenience* store nearby, because Kurt was craving marshmallows.

convince/persuade

You **convince** someone to believe; you **persuade** someone to act. Examples: By **convincing** me that the event would be fun, Ray **persuaded** me to go with him.

corporal/corporeal

A **corporal** is a noncommissioned officer in either the army or the marine corps; as an adjective, **corporal** means "relating to the body" (as in **corporal** punishment); it's also a cloth used in religious communion services. **Corporeal** means "relating to the physical rather than to the spiritual or abstract." Examples: When **Corporal** Mason barks an order, troops respond immediately. Mentally, I know I shouldn't be afraid, but my **corporal** mind knows that this vaccination will hurt! Hugging a tree can be both a **corporeal** and a spiritual experience, because touching it is physical, but the feeling can be spiritual.

corps/corpse

Corps (pronounced "core") is an organized branch of the military; a **corpse** is a dead body. Examples: The Army **Corps** of Engineers found the **corpse** of a deer in the woods.

couldn't care less

Couldn't care less is correct. This colloquial phrase should not be "could care less." Example: Carter **couldn't care less** about the paint spots on his jeans; he didn't think about them at all. (**Couldn't care less** is a British expression meaning "I have no interest in it whatsoever.")

"could of," "may of," "might of," "must of," "should of," "would of" (W.O.)

Use the verb *have*, not the preposition *of*, after verbs such as *could*, *should*, *would*, *may*, *might*, and *must*. Examples: They *must have* (not *must of*) left. I *may have* (not *may of*) lost the keys.

council/counsel

A *council* is a deliberative body, and a *councilor* is a member of that body. *Counsel* is a noun meaning "advice" and can also be another term for "lawyer"; as a verb it means "to give guidance and advice"; a *counselor* is one who gives advice. Examples: The *councilors* met to discuss the *council's* position on the matter. The pastor offered wise *counsel* to the young couple.

counterf<u>ei</u>t

This word means "not genuine; forged." Example: The kidnappers had been duped; the ransom money they were given was *counterfeit* and worth nothing. (See "ei" and "ie" section on page 201.)

"couple of," "couple a"

"Couple of" means "two," but it's not standard English. Don't use it in formal writing; use the word *two* — and never use "couple a."

c<u>our</u>teous

Think of being <u>*court*</u>*eous* in *court*.

coward/cowered

A *coward* is a person who is afraid; *cowered* is the past tense of the verb *to cower*, meaning "to back away or cringe in fear." Examples: The lion in *The Wizard of Oz* thought that he was a *coward*; he often *cowered* behind Dorothy.

craving/craving for

Use *craving* alone as the verb form; use *craving for* as a noun. It's incorrect to say, "I'm *craving for* some chocolate." Examples of correct usage: I am *craving* some dark chocolate! I have a *craving for* chocolate triangles with caramel centers.

credible/creditable

Credible means "believable"; *creditable* means "worthy of credit or praise." Examples: Eric's alibi was *credible*, so we realized he wasn't implicated in the case of the missing donuts. The soccer team played a *creditable* game and squeaked out a win in the last two minutes.

criteria, criterion

Criteria is the plural of *criterion*, which means "a standard, rule, or test on which a judgment or decision is made." Examples: The one *criterion* for the job was enthusiasm; there were other *criteria*. (Note that the verb must match the subject; *criteria* is plural, so the verb is *were*.)

criticism, criticize

Be careful of the change from *s* to *z*.

cruise

Beware of the silent *i*.

cue/queue

A *cue* is a clue or hint or a subtle pointing out of something; it's also a long, tapered stick used in playing billiards or pool; a *queue* (a term used mainly in Britain) is a file or line, especially of people awaiting their turn; it also is a braid of hair worn hanging down the back. Examples: Take a *cue* from Jeff; he's an accomplished pool player and often chalks his *cue*. Allison had a long braid of hair that draped down her back, and when she stood in line we joked that she was a girl with a *queue* in a *queue*!

cupidity

This noun has nothing to do with the cute little angel with the arrows who is particularly visible around Valentine's Day, Cupid. It means "excessive desire, especially desire for money." Example: Scrooge's *cupidity* forced him to think only of money and to miss out on love and compassion — until he changed his outlook.

data

The word **data** is the plural of **datum**, a piece of information, and the verb must agree with the plural form. Example: The **data** show (not shows) a rise in costs.

de<u>a</u>lt

This is the past tense of the verb **deal**. Example: Max **dealt** the cards with a flourish.

dec<u>ei</u>t, dec<u>ei</u>tful, dec<u>ei</u>ve

These words actually follow the "**i** before **e**" rule; check out the "ei" and "ie" section beginning on p. 201. **Deceit** is the act of cheating or committing fraud or trickery. Example: Edgardo's **deceit** forced his sister to marry someone she didn't love.

decent/descent/dissent

Decent is an adjective meaning "conforming to standards of moral behavior"; **descent** is a noun meaning "a fall, a decline, a way down." **To dissent** is a verb meaning "to disagree or differ" (<u>**dis**</u>sent and <u>**dis**</u>agree both begin with the same letters), or a noun meaning "a different opinion." Examples: His political **descent** from power was a result of his not being a **decent** senator, and because of his many **dissenting** votes against the majority.

decimate/disseminate

To decimate is to kill many of — literally, one in ten. **To disseminate** is to distribute or spread something, such as information or gossip. Examples: The workmen **decimated**

my petunias while clomping through the garden; many plants are crushed. I'm going to *disseminate* this information to the neighbors so these guys won't be hired again.

dec**i**sion

Remember *dec*, as in *dec**i**de*.

deduce/deduct/induce

To deduce is to come to a logical conclusion; *to deduct* means "to remove an amount." *To induce* is to bring on or encourage. Examples: From evidence he'd found, Sherlock Holmes would *deduce* who the murderer was. The contractor will *deduct* your deposit from the final bill. Sometimes doctors *induce* labor in their patients to make the birthing process shorter.

deference/difference

Deference is a noun meaning "courteous submission or yielding to the wishes, ideas, or opinions of others." *Difference* is the quality or condition of being unlike, different, or dissimilar; it also can mean "a change or effect." Examples: Jed's *deference* to my request that he eat more vegetables and fruits has made a *difference* in his overall health.

defic**i**ent, defic**i**ency, defic**i**encies

A *deficiency* is a lack of something essential in amount or degree. Example: If we don't get enough sunshine, we become *deficient* in vitamin D; I guess we'd better flee to Hawaii! (See "ei" and "ie" section on page 201.)

definitely, indefinitely (W.O.)

Fin and *finite* appear in both of these words. (Note: Your computer spell-checker may change *definitely* to *defiantly*, so don't trust it. Learn to spell the words instead!)

deify/deity

A *deity* is a god or goddess, and to *deify* is to make something or someone godlike. (See "ei" and "ie" section on page 201.)

deign

The word means "to condescend." Example: Marvin won't *deign* to hear my story; he says it isn't important. (See "ei" and "ie" section on page 201.)

demagogue/demigod

A *demagogue* is a political leader who appeals to followers' emotions and prejudices, rather than to their sense of reason. A *demigod* is someone treated as a god; it's also a minor god, or a being who is half human, half god. Examples: Many dictators are *demagogues* who foment revolution with fiery, emotional rhetoric. Some rock stars and popular athletes become virtual *demigods*, being treated with reverence and awe.

demur/demure

To demur is "to hesitate, to raise objections, or to challenge"; *demure* means "modest, shy, or prudish." Examples: The *demure* girl wanted to *demur*; skinny dipping was out of her comfort zone.

deprave/deprive

To deprave is to have a morally bad effect on someone; *to deprive* is to prevent somebody from having something. Examples: Some say that lewd, violent movies *deprave* children, which can *deprive* them of their innocence.

deprecate/depreciate

To deprecate is to express disapproval of; *to depreciate* is to undervalue or to lower in value. Examples: He *deprecated* me for buying the new car, scolding that it would *depreciate* in value immediately.

de<u>sc</u>endant

This word comes from *descend*, meaning "to go down, a way down, or to go down along a line, as a *descendant*." A *descendant* is a person, animal, or plant whose *descent* can be traced to a particular individual or group. Be careful to include *sc*; you can end the word in *ant* or *ent*.

desert/dessert

A *desert* is a barren wilderness; the verb *to desert* means "to leave somebody or something to whom or to which you have an obligation or duty." *Desert*, usually used in the plural form *deserts*, also refers to a punishment, as in: "The jailed sergeant got her just *deserts* for *deserting* her post." *Dessert*, with two *s*'s, is usually the final, sweet course of a meal, as in: "The *dessert* was warm <u>s</u>trawberry <u>s</u>hortcake, topped with frothy whipped cream and thick, dripping hot fudge."

DESERT

DESSERT

desperate/disparate

To be *desperate* is to be overwhelmed with urgency and anxiety, losing all hope; *disparate* describes people or things so different from each other that they cannot be compared. (Hint for spelling *desperate*: He was so hungry and *desper<u>ate</u>* that he *ate* anything he could find.)

develop

No *e* at the end of this word.

device/devise

A *device* is a noun meaning "a plan or scheme, a design, or a mechanical object"; *to devise* is a verb meaning "to plan" (these spellings are similar to those of **advice** and **advise**). Examples: You must **devise** a plan for us to use this kooky, odd, whimsical **device**!

diagnose

A disease is **diagnosed**; a patient is not. Examples: Micah's rash was **diagnosed** as poison oak; not: He was *diagnosed* with poison oak.

diagnosis/prognosis

A **diagnosis** is the decision reached in determining the nature or cause of a disease or injury; a **prognosis** is a forecast of the likelihood of recovery from a disease or something else. Examples: The **diagnosis** proved that Lyme disease was the culprit. Joe's **prognosis** was positive; he will recover fully, and so will the economy!

dialectic/dialect/didactic

Dialectic pertains to the art of arriving at a truth by the exchange of logical arguments. A **dialect** is a distinct type of language or expression associated with a specific region or social group. **Didactic** (also **didactical**) is an adjective that means "inclined to teach or moralize, often excessively." Examples: The conclusion was reached after the experts discussed the alternatives in a **dialectic** roundtable. Cajuns of Louisiana speak a lovely, melodious **dialect**. Professor Snarp tends to moralize and preach to his students in his **didactic** lectures.

dialog/dialogue

Either spelling is correct; a **dialog** is a conversation between two or more persons.

CAREFUL: THESE WORDS CAN BITE YOU!

Remember to include the following underlined letters:

ar<u>c</u>tic	colum<u>n</u>	ex<u>h</u>aust
bru<u>i</u>se	cru<u>i</u>se	lon<u>e</u>liness
busi<u>n</u>ess	de<u>a</u>lt	marri<u>a</u>ge
can<u>di</u>date	de<u>sc</u>endant	notic<u>e</u>able
carri<u>a</u>ge	dy<u>e</u>ing	panic<u>k</u>ing
chang<u>e</u>able	enviro<u>n</u>ment	picnic<u>k</u>ing

Don't add extra letters to these:

across...NOT ac<u>c</u>ross
among...NOT amo<u>u</u>ng
athlete...NOT ath<u>a</u>lete
bachelor...NOT ba<u>t</u>chelor
benefited...NOT benefi<u>t</u>ted
conceivable...NOT conceiv<u>e</u>able
convenient...NOT conv<u>i</u>enient
develop...NOT develop<u>e</u>
dining...NOT din<u>n</u>ing
disagree...NOT dis<u>s</u>agree
disastrous...NOT disast<u>e</u>rous
frustrated...NOT frust<u>e</u>rated
fulfill...NOT ful<u>l</u>fill
hindrance...NOT hind<u>e</u>rance
intriguing...NOT intrigu<u>e</u>ing
lining...NOT lin<u>n</u>ing
shining...NOT shin<u>n</u>ing
truly...NOT tru<u>e</u>ly
usage...NOT us<u>e</u>age
whining...NOT whin<u>n</u>ing

71

die/dying, dye/dyeing

Die, *dying*, and *dies* are forms of the verb meaning "to stop living"; *dye*, *dyeing*, and *dyes* refer to changing the color of something. (By the way, a *die* is one-half of a set of dice.) Examples: Jeanie's dream will *die* if she doesn't become an actor, so she *dyes* her hair before each audition to make it look fresh and trendy; her spare time is spent tie-*dyeing* beach towels to sell in Dana Point.

dietitian/politician

The first of these words has to do with food, and it's spelled with a **t**. Hint: Think of a *dietitian* drinking tea (both have *t*'s). *Politician*, however, is spelled with a **c**, as in *politics*.

differ from/ differ with

Differ from means "to be unlike"; *differ with* means "to disagree with." Examples: My class ring *differed from* Cathy's because the stones were not alike. Kelley *differed with* me about the decorations; she wanted flowers and I wanted balloons.

difficult/hard

Something that's *difficult* presents one or more problems; something *hard* is solid. While these words are also synonyms in certain contexts, the preferred word to mean "problematic" in formal writing is *difficult*. Examples: The hike was *difficult*, especially on the incline of *hard*, jarring clay.

dining

The *i* in dine is a long sound, so use only one *n* after it — the same as in *lining*, *mining*, *pining*, *shining*, *whining*.

CHEW ON THESE -CEEDS, -CEDES, AND -SEDES

These are "ceed" words:

exceed   succeed
proceed

These are "cede" words:

accede   intercede
antecede   precede
cede   recede
concede   secede

Here's a "sede" word:

supersede

disagree

One *s* only.

disappear, disappoint

One *s* and two *p*'s in these.

disastrous

No *e*. The word has three syllables and is not spelled "disasterous."

discover/invent

These are often used incorrectly: *to discover* is to notice, observe, or learn something for the first time; *to invent* is to produce or fabricate or contrive something using the imagination. Examples: Weyman **discovered** the problem by going back through the recipe; not enough saffron. Something new was **invented** in Silicon Valley that changed the world — it was a computer!

discreet/discrete

Discreet means "judicious or prudent"; *discrete* means "distinct, separate, diverse." Examples: Be **discreet** when you meet her boyfriend. Each cow has its own **discrete** markings.

disinterested/uninterested

Disinterested means "impartial and objective" (think: "<u>dis</u>tant"); *uninterested* means "not interested." Examples: Karen is a **disinterested** counselor who can be objective, not one who is **uninterested** in seeing that justice is done.

di<u>ss</u>atisfied

Remember, two *s*'s, one in each of the first two syllables.

di<u>ss</u>eminate

This word means "to distribute or spread something."

dive

In formal usage the past tense of **dive** is **dived**, not **dove**, as in: "He **dived** into the deep end of the pool." **Dove** (pronounced "duv") is a species of bird — or a brand of soap products or chocolate!

divest/invest/vested

To divest is to rid oneself of, to separate or dissociate from; **to invest** means "to put money to use for profitable returns," usually income or interest; the adjective **vested** describes something that's held completely, securely, and permanently, and that is protected or established as by right or law (think of keeping something in a vest pocket, close to you). Examples: We **divested** ourselves of many files when we cleaned the basement. We hope to **invest** wisely for our future. The owner had a **vested** interest in his company's success. The minister said, "By the authority **vested** in me, I pronounce you spouse and spouse!" (By the way, a **vest** is a sleeveless garment with buttons down the front, usually worn over a shirt or blouse.)

does/dose/doze

Does (pronounced "duz") is the present tense of the verb **to do**. *Does* ("dōz") is also the plural of **doe**, a female deer, kangaroo, goat, rabbit, and so on. **Dose** ("dōs") is an amount of something to be consumed, often for treatment of a malady. *To doze* is to sleep lightly. Examples: She **does** her work. Take a small **dose** of aspirin tonight. Don't **doze** in class; it **does** not please the teacher.

done/finished/through

In a formal context, **done** means "to be cooked thoroughly," while *finished* indicates that something has been completed, as in: "The roast is **done**, and I have **finished** reading the paper." Don't phrase it this way: "I'm done reading the paper." Similarly, say, "I'm **finished** reading this," not "I'm *through* reading it."

dramatic/traumatic

Dramatic means "expressive through emotion or action," and it relates to the theater, as in: "*La Bohème* is a *dramatic* and emotional opera by Giacomo Puccini." *Traumatic* refers to a shock or injury to the mind or body that causes major distress. For example: The hurricane and its aftermath were a *traumatic* and cataclysmic occurrence.

dreamed/dreamt

Either is correct. *Dreamt* is reportedly the only word in the English language that ends in *mt*. These two words are the past tense of the verb *to dream*.

dr<u>ei</u>del

A *dreidel* is a four-sided top bearing Hebrew letters and is used as a toy, especially around the time of Hanukkah. (See "ei" and "ie" section on page 201.)

dual/duel

Dual is an adjective meaning "of two, or double." The noun *duel* is a planned, formal fight between two armed persons; the verb *to duel* means "to fight a duel for one's honor." (Think: Justice is <u>due</u>, so there will be a <u>duel</u>.)

DUAL / DUEL

due to

Due to is a modifying (adjective) phrase; don't use it to mean "because of." Use **due to** following forms of the verb *to be*. Examples: Ali's great success was **due to** her diligence and hard work. The play was canceled **because of** (not *due to*) the illness of the actors.

each, either (W.O.)

Each is singular; so is *either*. Examples: **Each has** (not *have*) **his** or **her** (not *their*) own idea. **Either** of the flavors **is** (not *are*) fine with me. (If you have trouble remembering this, add a mental *one*: **Each one has his** or **her** passion.)

each other/one another

This is a two-word term — it's not spelled "eachother." Also, use **each other** when referring to two; **one another** applies to three or more. Examples: You two be nice to **each other**. The children exchanged the gifts among **one another**.

Earth/earth

Capitalize the word **Earth** when referring to the planet; don't capitalize it when the word refers to dirt or soil.

economic/economical

The word **economic** pertains to an economy, or to the production, development, and management of material wealth, or to the science of economics. **Economical** means "prudent, thrifty, and wise in managing, particularly with money or resources." Examples: The stock market goes through **economic** fluctuations constantly. Shauna is **economical** in using office supplies, recycling whenever she can.

ec<u>s</u>ta<u>s</u>y

There's no *x* in this word. And there are two **s**'s, rather than two *c*'s.

effic<u>ie</u>nt, effic<u>ie</u>ncy

(See "ei" and "ie" section on page 201.)

e.g./etc./i.e.

The abbreviation *e.g.* comes from **exempli gratia** and means "for example." The abbreviation *etc.* comes from **et cetera** and means "and so forth" or "and so on." And *i.e.* comes from **id est**, meaning "that is." Don't use these abbreviations in formal writing, however, and never use the phrase "and et cetera," as that's redundant. One last thing: note that **et cetera** has no *k* sound; don't say "e<u>k</u>setera."

either/or, neither/nor

Either goes with *or*, and *neither* goes with *nor*. Examples: *Either* you're in *or* you're not. *Neither* the dog *nor* the cat has fleas.

elder/older

Elder as a description indicates seniority between two people, especially siblings; *elder* used as a noun denotes one older or higher in rank in a tribe or organization, as in: "the church *elders*." *Older* is a comparative of *old*, and it means "having greater age than someone else." Examples: The *elder* brother became king. Consuela is *older* than Marianne by two years.

elicit/illicit

To elicit means "to bring out, to evoke"; *illicit* means "unlawful, illegal." Examples: I was not able to *elicit* information from the press about the *illicit* money-laundering case. (Hint: Think of "ill" and i<u>ll</u>egal, which have negative connotations.)

eli<u>gi</u>ble

No *a*.

ellipsis mark

An ellipsis mark is three dots (...) indicating that some text has been omitted from a quotation. An ellipsis is also used to show where a thought trails off, or where speech drifts off, as when one is musing or is interrupted. Sometimes in quotations, four dots (including the period) are used to show that text has been omitted from the end of a sentence — but never use more than four dots.

emba<u>rr</u><u>ass</u>

Two *r*'s and two *s*'s.

emigrate from/immigrate to

Notice that one of these terms has one *m* and the other has two. *To emigrate* is to leave one country to live in another; *to immigrate* is to enter another country and reside there. Examples: The family left; they **emigrated** from France to find work, and they **immigrated** to Spain, where they settled. (Hint: **Emigrate** and *exit* both begin with *e*. Note: An **emigrant** leaves his or her country; an **immigrant** comes to one country from another.)

eminent/imminent

Eminent means "distinguished or superior"; *imminent* means "impending, sure to happen." Also, **eminent domain** is the right of a government to take over private property for public use. Examples: The rain was **imminent**; it would arrive soon, soaking the **eminent** dignitaries on the stage. (Think of **imminent** and _impending_, which both begin with the same letters.)

ending sentences with prepositions

An argument exists that it's not correct to end a sentence with a preposition (see "The Parts of Speech" section near the start of the book). Adherence to this rule is dwindling; for instance, while it is correct to say "For whom will you vote?," most agree that asking "Whom will you vote for?" is acceptable. That said, be aware of this rule and follow it when you can. Don't say, for instance: "Where are you going to?" "Where did you buy that at?" "What time should we be home by?" In these cases, you can simply drop the *to*, *at*, or *by* at the end of the sentences. And be very clear with your use of prepositions, no matter where they appear in a sentence. To further illustrate my point, I hope you'll enjoy this hilarious unattributed sentence from Wikipedia: "The little boy says to his father, 'Daddy, what did you bring that book that I don't want to be read to out of up for?' "

enormity/enormousness

Enormity is extreme evil or offensiveness; *enormousness* refers to the quality of being very large, or huge, in size or capacity. Examples: Neighbors were aghast at the *enormity* of the crime. The *enormousness* of the blimp hangar amazed us.

enrage/outrage

To enrage means "to infuriate or put into a rage"; *to outrage* is to subject to grievous violence or indignity. The noun *outrage* is an act of wanton violence or a violation of the laws of decency. Examples: The lack of input in government decisions can *enrage* the populace. That the rapist was acquitted by the judge is an *outrage*. We were *outraged* and embarrassed when Annie called us liars in front of our friends.

envelop/envelope

To envelop is to surround, wrap, or encapsulate; an *envelope* is a flat paper container with a closure. Examples:

David will **envelop** us in sensuous jazz while we stuff **envelopes** for the concert.

environment

Don't forget the **n** in the middle.

epiphany/epitome

An **epiphany** is a sudden realization or comprehension, an "aha moment"; capitalized, it is also a Christian feast on January 6. An **epitome** (pronounced "e-pit'-oh-me") describes a person or thing that is typical or that possesses to a high degree the features of an entire class. Examples: Geri had an **epiphany** when she realized she actually was in love! Eric and Lisa are the **epitome** of a happily married couple.

equable/equitable

Equable means "calm and even-tempered"; **equitable** means "just and fair." Examples: Judge Horton was **equable** and personable; and when she was working in court, she was fair and **equitable**.

equation

It's not spelled "sion" — the word comes from **equate**.

erotic/erratic

The word **erotic** concerns lust, sexual love, or desire; **erratic** means "having no steady, fixed course or lacking consistency." Examples: Films rated X often are **erotic** in nature. Gabe's academic habits are **erratic**; sometimes he studies until midnight, and other times not at all.

especially

It's spelled **e_specially**; don't pronounce it "e_xpecially."

eventually/ultimately

Eventually means "at an unspecified time in the future"; *ultimately* means "in the end." Examples: We'd hoped to win a game **eventually**, but **ultimately** we took the championship!

every day/everyday

Every day is a combination of the adjective **every** and the noun **day**, and it states when something happens or is done, as in: "Ashley tends her garden **every day**." The word **everyday** is an adjective: "It was an **everyday** occurrence."

everyone/every one

Everyone is a pronoun meaning "all"; *every one* means "each person or thing." Examples: **Everyone** at the party took **every one** of the table decorations.

every time

This term is two words, not one. Example: **Every time** I see you, I have to smile.

everywhere

It's one word, not two. Example: **Everywhere** you go you bring happiness!

exalt/exult

To exalt is to raise somebody or something in position, rank, or esteem, or to praise highly; *to exult* is to rejoice. Examples: We *exult* in your great victory. We *exalt* you, and we're giving you the trophy because you've really impressed us.

excuse/recuse

To excuse is a verb meaning "to release somebody from doing something" (as in: "I will *excuse* you from doing your homework tonight") or "to release from blame or criticism for a mistake or wrongdoing" (as in: "I hope Mom will *excuse* me for eating the last cupcake; I was starving!"). The noun *excuse* is a justification, a reason, or an explanation that may not be true. The verb *to recuse* is to disqualify someone from judging or participating in something because of possible personal bias or interest: "Judge Martin *recused* himself from the case because he had stock in the allegedly fraudulent company."

exercise/exorcise

Exercise is physical activity; *to exercise* means "to do physical activity for health and fitness" or "to practice a skill or behavior." *To exorcise* is to free someone or something from evil, or to send evil away. Examples: Clare *exercised* by walking each day. In the film *The Exorcist*, the devil was *exorcised* from the soul and body of the little girl.

exhaust

Don't forget the *h*; it's silent.

existence

The end of the word is spelled **_ence_**; there's no **a** in it.

existent/extant/extent

Existent means "real or actual, not imagined or invented," as in: "The rules are *existent* for a reason; follow them!" *Extant* means "still in existence," as in: "Fortunately, a copy of the rare book is *extant*; it's the only one on the planet." An *extent* is a length or amount: "Let's survey the *extent* of the fire's damage."

HOW MANY LEGS? ANTENNAE? WINGS? STINGERS?

Use these with quantities that cannot be counted:

amount	less
further	much

When talking about numbers, use these with quantities that can be counted:

farther	many
fewer	number

---

expansive/expensive

Expansive is an adjective that means "large in size or extent, and capable of growing larger"; *expensive* means "costing a large amount of money." Examples: Because of her new career as an executive, Sharon was given an **expansive** credit card limit. She began shopping in exclusive stores that sold **expensive** items.

explicit/implicit

Explicit describes something expressed directly or clearly defined; *implicit* means "implied or unstated." Examples: Although I gave my brother **explicit** instructions to get home early, he was late anyway. Dad's silent scowl showed **implicit** disapproval.

faint/feint

Faint, as an adjective, means "weak," and the verb **to faint** means "to collapse without strength." (Hint: If you <u>fa</u>int, you might <u>fa</u>ll.) A **feint** is a deceptive move to divert attention. Examples: Danisha will **faint** when she sees the deceptive **feint** her friend devised to get her to the surprise birthday party! (See "ei" and "ie" section on page 201.)

fallow/follow

Fallow means "uncultivated, unplanted, or unseeded"; *follow* means "to come after or behind." Examples: *Follow* me to the old *fallow* field, where nothing grows.

fam<u>ili</u>ar

fanc<u>ie</u>d, fanc<u>ie</u>r, fanc<u>ie</u>s

To fancy is to like, or to visualize, imagine, or suppose. Examples: Cameron is a **fancier** of fine wines, and he particularly **fancies** the reds from the northern area of Napa County. (See "ei" and "ie" section on page 201.)

farther/further

Traditionally, *farther* describes physical, countable space or distance; *further* suggests an additional, or uncountable, quantity or degree. Examples: Ercoli threw the ball ten feet *farther* than anyone else. Elle will give you *further* information for the treasure hunt once you figure out this clue.

faze/phase

To faze means "to upset or disrupt the composure of someone or something"; the noun *phase* is a specific stage of development, and the verb, usually used with *out* or *in*, means "to do something systematically by stages." Examples: Josh was going through a typical teen *phase* and would soon grow out of it, so his parents weren't *fazed* by his behavior. We *phased in* the new program a little at a time.

feign/fain

Feign means "to put on a fictitious appearance" or "to make up excuses." *Fain*, a term more common in archaic works, means "gladly or willingly." Examples: Corrina will *feign* boredom and insouciance at the reception, but in reality, she is merely shy. "I *fain* wouldst go to the ball with you," exclaimed Clark. (See "ei" and "ie" section on page 201.)

feisty

To be *feisty* is to be lively, spirited, aggressive, or quick tempered. Example: The *feisty* little calico kitten shredded the entire comics section of the Sunday paper. (See "ei" and "ie" section on page 201.)

ferment/foment

To ferment is to produce through a state of agitation or turbulence. *Fermentation* is part of the process of alcohol manufacturing; as a noun, *ferment* is what causes the change. *To foment* is similar but more often is used in reference to what people do to incite or stir up, or to promote the growth of something. Examples: Winemakers usually *ferment* chardonnay grapes in oak barrels to produce the luscious white wine. Vance tried to *foment* interest in his project to start a band; he sent text messages to his old musician friends.

fêted/fetid

To fête is to honor someone with a celebration in his or her name (a *fête* is the celebration); the adjective *fetid* means "having a foul odor; stinking." Examples: Victoria will be *fêted* with a lavish soiree on her eighteenth birthday; I hope it won't be held near the *fetid*, smelly swamp at the rear of the mansion.

fewer/less (W.O.)

Fewer refers to items that can be counted; *less* refers to general amounts. Examples: *Fewer* people seem to work out and run in the Midwest, but there is *less* stress within the populace of the heartland, according to some studies.

fiancé, fiancée

These terms are used to denote persons who are engaged to be married; an engaged man is a *fiancé*, and an engaged woman is a *fiancée* (both are pronounced "fee-on'-say").

fi**er**y

This describes something afire or engulfed in flames; be careful not to write "firey."

filial/finial

Filial relates to a son or daughter; a *finial* is a decorative top piece that secures a lampshade onto a lamp. Examples: *Filial* duties include always remembering Mother's Day and Father's Day! The *finial* holding the green shade onto the lamp is a deep emerald color.

finale/finally

Finale (pronounced "fin-a'-lay") denotes the concluding portion, especially of a musical composition. *Finally* (pronounced "fy'-nal-lee") is from the same root word, *final*, but it is an adverb meaning "at the final or last point or moment" or "in a final manner; conclusively or decisively." Examples: By the *finale* of the concert, the adults had *finally* had enough of punk rock!

financ**ie**r

A *financier* is one who is expert in large-scale financial affairs. (See "ei" and "ie" section on page 201.)

"first annual"

This incorrect term describes an impossible circumstance; if something is happening for the first time, it can't be an annual occurrence — at least not until the second year.

"firstly"

This is pretentious and leads to an awkward series: *firstly, secondly, thirdly*. It's better to use **first**, **second**, **third** instead.

fiscal/physical

Fiscal means "of or relating to expenditures, revenues, or debt" — that is, finance or finances, as in a **fiscal** policy for a corporation. **Physical** has to do with the body, as opposed to the mind or spirit. Examples: Lloyd's company's **fiscal** calendar went from June of one year through May of the following year. Hui believes that **physical** fitness is as important as mental discipline.

flammable/inflammable

These two words, oddly, have the same meaning: "easily set on fire; combustible."

flaunt/flout/flautist

To flaunt is to show something off or to parade ostentatiously; **to flout** is to scorn by disobeying or defying. A **flautist** (also called a flutist) is one who plays a flute. Examples: Peacocks **flaunt** their stunning blue-green feathers; of course, they are males! Don't try to **flout** my authority; after all, I'm the babysitter here.

flotsam/jetsam

While these are similar, **flotsam** is wreckage or cargo floating in the water after a ship has sunk; **jetsam** is cargo or equipment purposely tossed overboard, or jettisoned, to lighten a ship in distress.

folks

This is an informal word for family or for people in general; don't use it in formal writing or speaking. Example: My **family** (not *folks*) will be here for the holidays.

forbear/forebear

To **forbear** is to tolerate with great patience or to abstain; a **forebear** is an ancestor. Examples: We will **forbear** the long, dusty road to see the lions. Lotte's **forebears** emigrated from Denmark. (Think: **Forebears** came be<u>fore</u>.)

for<u>ei</u>gn

Hint: Royalty <u>reign</u>s in some **for<u>ei</u>gn** countries. (See "ei" and "ie" section on page 201.)

foreword/forward

A **foreword** is in the front part of a book and gives the reader introductory remarks about it. **Forward** means "directed or moving toward the front"; it also can refer to bold, aggressive action. Examples: The **foreword** of the book tells what the reader can expect inside. This one, *The Bugaboo Review*, should move you **forward** on your quest toward excellence in the use of the English language — is it too **forward** of me to say so?

forf<u>ei</u>t

To forfeit means "to surrender something as a punishment for a crime, error, or breach of contract." Example: Roderick had to **forfeit** his deposit on the rental because his brother had broken a window with his violin bow. (See "ei" and "ie" section on page 201.)

formally/formerly

Formally means "something done in a formal, convention-ally correct manner"; *formerly* refers to a previous time. Examples: Elaine and Bob were *formally* introduced at the meeting, but then they realized that they had *formerly* met at the university.

fort/forte

A *fort* is a place of fortification or strength, such as an army post; *forte* (pronounced "fort," not "for'-tay") is the French word for "strong" and names something at which one excels. In music, the Italian pronunciation, "for'-tay," is used, as much music is influenced by the Italian language. Examples: The "Dies Irae" in Verdi's *Requiem* is played *forte*; its sudden, loud intensity often frightens the unaware! Adriana and Tamara built a *fort* of sheets in the living room. Public speaking is McKay's *forte*; he does it very well.

forty/fourth/forth

Forty and *fourth* have to do with numbers; *forth* is an adverb meaning, "forward, ahead, abroad." Examples: Elena lived at *Forty-Fourth* Street and *Fourth* Avenue. Go *forth* and prosper!

found

This word has several different meanings. It is the past tense of *to find*, which means "to locate or come upon." *To found* means "to establish or set up, especially with a provision for continual existence." Examples: Hunter *found* Amy's keys in his pocket. Taft wants to *found* a boys' club in his neighborhood.

freight

(See "ei" and "ie" section on page 201.)

frustrated/flustered

Don't add an extra *e* — it's not spelled "frusterated" — and it certainly is not "flustrated," a combination of *frustrated* and *flustered*. *Frustrated* means "being thwarted, invalidated, or nullified, or prevented from accomplishing a purpose or fulfilling a desire"; *flustered* means "nervous, flummoxed, upset, agitated, or excited." Examples: Ali was *flustered* to find she had grabbed the little pitcher of soy sauce for her coffee, instead of the creamer; what a gustatory disaster! Bron was *frustrated* that he hadn't had enough time to finish the test.

fulfill

Don't add an extra *l*. It's not spelled "fullfill."

gage/gauge/gouge

Gage and *gauge* (both pronounced "gayge") mean "to measure," or are a standard of measurement or a device used to measure. Less common, a *gage* is a pledge, something deposited or given as security against an obligation. *To gouge* (pronounced "gowge") is to scoop or dig out, as with a chisel, or to extort for money. Examples: We *gauged* the time to be about 7:45 when the swindler *gouged* us for parking: forty-three dollars for six minutes!

gait/gate

A *gait* is a manner of walking, running, or moving along on foot; a *gate* is a movable barrier, usually on hinges, that closes a gap in a fence or wall. Examples: The runner's *gait* was smooth and steady, and she won the race after charging through the final *gate* in the meadow run.

gall/Gaul

Gall is bitterness of feeling, rancor, something vexing, irritating, or bitter to endure; it is also outrageous insolence. The verb *to gall* means to make sore or to vex or irritate, or to be or become chafed. *Gaul* (it's capitalized) is a Celt of the ancient land of Gaul, a French person, or an ancient region of western Europe. Examples: It took a lot of *gall* for the upset parent to chastise the teacher. The novice cowboy became *galled* and chapped from riding the horse; he could barely walk the next day.

gamble/gambol

To gamble is to play games that involve risking money, or to bet on the outcome of an event or competition; *to gambol* is to leap or skip about playfully. Examples:

Devon **gamboled** all around the casino when her five-dollar **gamble** on the horse race paid off.

gargle/gargoyle

To gargle is "to force exhaled air through a liquid in the back of the mouth, with head tilted back"; a **gargoyle** is a grotesquely carved figure of a human or animal, often seen as a spout that drains rainwater from a roof into a gutter. Examples: It sounded as if the **gargoyles** were **gargling** as they spewed rain from the roof of the cathedral.

geisha

A **geisha** is a Japanese girl or woman trained in the arts as a companion for men. (See "ei" and "ie" section on page 201.)

gerund form using the possessive

A gerund is formed by adding **ing** to a verb and treating it as a noun, as in: "Your **dancing** makes me very happy." In this case **dancing** is the gerund. **Dance + ing**, the subject of the sentence, is a noun, so it calls for a possessive pronoun preceding it, as does any noun: "your" rather than "you"; "your dancing," not "you dancing." Some more examples: **My** giving (not *Me giving*) you the doll was a choice I made. **His** lying (not *Him lying*) is hateful. (Note: If you have trouble getting this, remember that gerunds are just like any noun that shows ownership or possession: *Angelina's* doll, *his* hateful lies, the *cat's* toy, *your* crying, *Monica's* whining, *Jarvis's* playing.)

gild/guild

To gild is to coat with a thin layer of gold; a **guild** is an association of people with similar interests. Examples:

Workers will **gild** some of the architectural details in the reconstruction of San Francisco's opera house so it retains its original gold look. **Guilds**, supportive organizations for workers, were precursors to today's unions.

THE "ROACH MOTELS" OF THE ENGLISH LANGUAGE: DON'T GO THERE!

Don't misuse **of**. *Use the verb* **have**, *not the preposition* **of**, *after verbs such as* **could, should, would, may, might**, *and* **must**. *For example, say:*

could have, NOT *could of*
might have, NOT *might of*

If it doesn't add meaning, don't add **of**:

inside, NOT *inside of*
off, NOT *off of*

Don't misuse **where** *by substituting it for* **that** *or* **in which**. *Say:*

I heard **that** (NOT *where*) the crime rate is increasing.
It is a story **in which** (NOT *where*) the children solve the mystery.

gilt/guilt

The noun **gilt** is a thin layer of gold, or goldlike substance, that is applied in the gilding process (see **gild**); it is also a superficial brightness or gloss. **Guilt** is being culpable for a crime or offense, or it is the remorse one feels for having committed something wrong. Examples: Dominic wanted to put **gilt** on the antique desk, but its pristine naturalness was much more beautiful. Richard harbored much **guilt** for having waited such a long time to call.

glacier

A **glacier** is a gigantic mass of ice slowly moving over a landmass. (See "ei" and "ie" section on page 201.)

gluten/glutton

Gluten is a mixture of plant proteins in cereal, especially wheat; a **glutton** is one who overeats or drinks too much.

good/well (W.O.)

Good is an adjective and describes a noun or pronoun; **well** is an adverb and describes a verb, an adjective, or another adverb, as in: "Alyssa did a **good** job planting the garden, and the flowers grew **well**." **Good** (an adjective) describes *job* (a thing, a noun); **well** (an adverb) describes *how* the flowers *grew* (a verb, which shows action, in this case).

gored/gourd

Gored, a verb in the past tense, means "pierced with the horns of an animal" (**gore** is the clotted blood it produces — ugh!); as an adjective, **gored** describes a sail, skirt, or the like that has one or more triangular pieces of fabric, called **gores**, inserted into it. A **gourd** is a member of the squash family; sometimes the dried form is made into a utensil for scooping. Examples: Samantha wore a **gored** skirt to the bullring, where she hoped nobody would be **gored** by the bull! We put out colorful, decorative **gourds** during fall.

gourmand/gourmet

A **gourmand** is a glutton, an overeater; a **gourmet** is someone who appreciates and enjoys good food. **Gourmet** is also an adjective, as in: "Benissimo Restaurant serves simple **gourmet** Italian food; *benissimo* means 'very, very fine,' so of course the food is delicious!"

grammar

It's spelled **grammar**, with an a, not "grammer."

grateful

It's spelled with **grate**, not "great."

guidance

It's spelled with **ance**, not "ence." Think of being guided on the **dance** floor.

"hadn't ought"

This is incorrect — instead say, **You ought not** or **You shouldn't**.

hallow/hollow

To hallow is to make something or somebody holy, or to respect or revere someone or something; **hollow** means "having an empty area inside," or "not solid"; it also means "insincere." Examples: The priestess will **hallow** the sacred ground of her people. The pumpkin was **hollow** after having been turned into a jack-o'-lantern. Ed's was a **hollow** compliment; he didn't mean it at all.

hand out/handout

To hand out is to give something, often free; a **handout** is a leaflet or flyer given out to announce an event or the like, or it is food, clothing, money given to the needy. Examples: Here's the **handout** for Friday's concert; the staff will **hand out** T-shirts to the first fifty people to arrive.

hanged/hung

Hanged is the past tense of the verb **to hang** when it means "to execute by hanging by the neck." *Hung* is the past tense and past participle of the verb **to hang** when it means "to fasten or to suspend." Examples: The prisoner was **hanged** at dawn. The stockings were **hung** (not *hanged*) by the chimney with care.

hang out/hangout

To hang out is slang for getting together with friends; a **hangout** is a frequently visited or favorite place. Examples: Reid and Matt like to **hang out** at the gym; it's the favorite **hangout** of many teens.

harass

Remember, it's spelled with one *r*. *To harass* is to bother, attack, or annoy someone persistently. Example: Lucinda would **harass** and bully the new freshman until the teacher stepped in.

hardly

Hardly means "barely, almost not at all" or "with great difficulty." Don't use it with a negative. Examples: We **could** (not *couldn't*) **hardly** hear the play. We **can** (not *can't*) **hardly** believe our good fortune!

"has got," "have got"

Got is unnecessary and awkward, and it should not be used in this context. Example: We **have** (not *We have got* or *We've got*) three days to finish this job.

"have went"

This is incorrect; instead, write: **should/would/could have gone**. Example: Holly **should have gone** (not *should have went*) to the bank before it closed.

he/she, his/her

While we are politically correct in including both sexes, this form, with the slash, is awkward and should not be used in formal writing. Instead, use **he or she**, **her or his**. However, don't use them too often; rewrite your sentence some other way, using, for instance, *people* or other plural nouns or pronouns, or an article instead of a pronoun. Examples: **Each** of the guests gave **his or her** opinion. **All** of the guests gave **their** opinions. **People** gave **their** opinions. **Each** guest gave **an** opinion.

FEED THESE TO THE BUG ZAPPER

These should not be used in sophisticated writing or speaking:

all's	boughten	nother
alot	irregardless	nowheres
anyways	kinda	orientate
anywheres	muchly	prophesize

These terms are nonstandard; don't use them in formal writing, in intellectual dialogue, or during a job interview!

all the farther	I feel like that	off of
alright	we should	o.k.
angry at	I see what	okay
being as how	you're	over with
being that	saying	reason…is
can't barely	is when	because
can't get no	is where	should have
can't hardly	is…is	went
could have	keep on	sort of
went	kind of	sure and
couldn't hardly	landed up	these ones
hadn't ought	later on	try and
has got	like how	up till
have got	like that we	up until
how about we	lots	whole nother
in between	lots of	
in regards to		

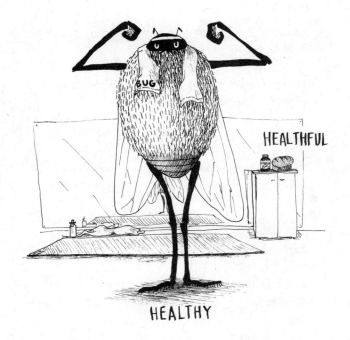

HEALTHFUL

HEALTHY

healthful/healthy

Healthful means "beneficial to health, or wholesome"; *healthy* means "robust, well, hearty." If you say that the wheat bread is "healthy," it means that the bread is *in* good health (as if it had been working out!), not that it is good *for* one's health.

hear/here

To hear is a verb meaning "to detect sound through the ear." *Here* is an adverb telling where. (Hint: The word *ear* is in the word *hear*, which you do with your ear!) Examples: Did Patrick *hear* me when I said, "Come *here*!"?

heard/herd

Heard is the past tense of *to hear*, meaning "to perceive through the ear." A *herd* is a gathering of animals of one species, and the term is sometimes used to refer to people; *to herd* is a verb meaning "to gather species into a group." Examples: Emily *heard* the thundering *herd* of Cape buffalo when she visited Kenya during her Semester at Sea educational voyage.

h<u>ei</u>fer

A *heifer* is a cow under three years of age that has not produced a calf. (See "ei" and "ie" section on page 201.)

h<u>eigh</u>t

Both the spelling and the pronunciation of this word can be tricky (no *h* at the end as there is in *width*); it's pronounced "hite." (See "ei" and "ie" section on page 201.)

h<u>ei</u>nous

Heinous means "hateful, odious, abominable." (See "ei" and "ie" section on page 201.)

h<u>ei</u>r, h<u>ei</u>ress, h<u>ei</u>rloom

An *heir* or *heiress* is one who inherits the property, title, or possessions of another. An *heirloom* is an item of value handed down to *heirs* through generations. Example: Sophia inherited the gold *heirloom* locket from her mother, who had received it from *her* grandmother. (See "ei" and "ie" section on page 201.)

heist

A *heist* is slang meaning "a robbery or burglary"; the verb *to heist* means "to rob or steal." (See "ei" and "ie" section on page 201.)

herein

Herein means "in or into this place." Example: *Herein* lies the problem: the key doesn't fit the lock! (See "ei" and "ie" section on page 201.)

"him and I went," "her and I talked," "him and me saw it," "me and Paolo did it," "Lan and him ate" — *and any similar example of a compound subject* (W.O.)

These are *incorrect*! To check yourself, mentally take one of the subjects away and hear how juvenile the sentence sounds: *him* went…*her* talked…*me* saw it…*me* did it…*him* ate. Say instead: *He* and *I* went (he went, and I went). *She* and *I* talked (she talked, and I talked). Lan and *he* ate (Lan ate, and he ate). Paolo and I sang (Paolo sang, and I sang).

hindrance

Though derived from the word *hinder*, it's only two syllables, with no *e* in the middle.

hippie/hippy

Hippie refers to the flower children of the 1960s. *Hippy* describes one who has large hips, but the word has morphed to the point that it sometimes is used when referring to *hippies*. Examples: *Hippies* gathered at the corner of Haight and Ashbury Streets in San Francisco. The actress was curvaceous and *hippy*.

HIPPIE   HIPPY

historic/historical

Historic and *historical* are similar, but a distinction exists. *Historic* refers to what is important in history, such as the *historic* flight of Lindbergh. It is also used for something that is famous or interesting due to its association with persons or events in history, such as Jefferson's *historic* home, Monticello. *Historical* refers to what has existed in the past, whether important or not, such as a minor *historical* incident. *Historical* also refers to anything dealing with history or the study of the past, such as Lincoln's *historical* address, or *historical* discoveries. While these distinctions are helpful, the words are often used interchangeably, as in: "*historic* times or *historical* times."

hoard/horde

To hoard is to collect a large amount of something, often in secret; the noun *hoard* means "a cache or a supply of something saved for the future." A *horde* is a large group of living things, such as people, animals, insects, or the like. Thus, *hoard* refers to things, items, or objects; *horde* applies to living beings, generally. Examples: When people began to *hoard* pennies, there was a shortage for general use, and it seems *hordes* of people did that. A *horde* of locusts destroyed all the crops in the region. (Hint: Hide your *hoard* under a b<u>oard</u>.)

hoarse/horse

Hoarse describes a condition of the throat in which the voice has a grating or husky sound; a *horse* is a four-footed animal with a mane and long tail. Examples: Lauren became *hoarse* after yelling for her *horse* to win the race.

holed up/hold up/holdup

The slang term *holed up* means "hidden out, concealed, or lying low," as in: "Brad was *holed up* in the library, studying the newest medical journal." *Hold up* (two words) has several meanings: "to assist or support" ("Kent will *hold up* Kendra if she ever falters"); "to delay or hinder" ("If you *hold up* the group any longer, we will be late!"); "to elevate" ("Carlos wants to *hold up* a sign saying, 'Go, Arcadia!'"); and "to rob" ("The boys wanted to *hold up* the girls at the bake sale, demanding cookies"). A *holdup* (one word) is a robbery, heist, or theft. Example: The girls were wise to the little robbers and hid the cookies before the hungry thieves arrived for the *holdup*. (Note: The terms *holed up*, *hold up*, and *holdup* are colloquial and shouldn't be used formally.)

holy/holey/wholly

Holy means "sacred" or refers to a divine power; *holey* describes something that is full of holes, such as a teen's jeans or Swiss cheese; *wholly* means "completely, entirely, or exclusively." Examples: Many people consider houses of worship — such as churches, cathedrals, mosques, temples, Kingdom Halls, and synagogues — to be *holy*; nonbelievers don't *wholly* agree with that description.

hopefully

This is an adverb, and it means "with hope or in a hopeful manner," as in: "Tina looked *hopefully* toward the door." Don't use it as follows: "*Hopefully*, the sun will shine today." Instead, show who's doing the hoping (the preceding example implies that the sun is hoping), or use *it is hoped*, or *I hope*, or *we hope*. For example, say: "She asked *hopefully* if her son would recover soon" or "*We hope* the sun will finally shine today." Do the same with other adverbs, such as *sadly*, *happily*, *frankly*, *honestly*, and *seriously*. Use them to describe the verb.

"How about we..."

This is an incorrect formation of a question; it is better to add *if*, as in: "*How about if* we go there instead?" Or, better yet: "*What if* we go the movies instead?"

hyper/hypo

The prefix *hyper* means "over, or more"; *hypo* means "under, or less." Examples: The *hyper*active child was even livelier when she was itching and needed to use *hypo*allergenic lotions and soaps. (Think: The *hypo* hippo went "under" the water! The *hyper* hyena never stopped pacing around the encampment; his constant movement made us nervous.)

hyphens, briefly

Remember to use hyphens when you make one word out of several: *sister-in-law*, *one-of-a-kind*, *mother-of-pearl*, *one-sided*, a *spare-the-air* day. Hyphenate certain compound descriptive words when they precede the noun they describe, but not when they appear after it: The *cone-shaped* hat was kitschy; the kitschy hat was *cone shaped*. The *icicle-laden* tree was glistening in the light; the tree glistening in the light was *laden with icicles*.

idle/idol

Idle is an adjective that means "inactive, not moving, lazy"; the noun *idol* describes something worshipped or revered, an image or icon. Examples: As the old English proverb says, "*Idle* hands are the Devil's workshop." Elvis is her *idol*; she nearly worships him.

if/whether

If signals general speculation or wondering; *whether* is used when two alternatives are present, or when the second is understood. Examples: I wonder *if* Arlene is lost. I wonder *whether* she's lost or just lollygagging. See *whether* she's lost. (Note: Generally, when you use *whether*, don't add "or not": it's implied in the context.)

"I feel like that we should..."

This is incorrect; it has too many words in it! Instead say, "*I feel we should...*," or simply, "*We should...*"

TWO BUGS OR ONE?

These terms are two words:

all right	each other
a lot	every time

These terms are one word:

everywhere	something
nevertheless	throughout
somebody	without
someone	

if...were

Under certain conditions, signaled by the word *if*, use **were** instead of *was*. Examples: *If* I **were** (not *was*) you, I wouldn't do that. *If* he **were** to leave now, he'd be early. *If* she **were** late, she'd be in trouble. "*If* I **were** a rich man..."

immoral/immortal

Immoral means "going against established moral rules or principles"; *immortal* means "not able to die, or everlasting." Examples: Certain **immoral** acts include rape and incest. Greek and Roman gods were considered **immortal** and could escape death.

immortal/invincible

Immortal means "everlasting or not subject to dying," or "enduring forever"; *invincible* means "unconquerable, not able to be defeated or overcome."

imply/infer

Imply means "to suggest or state indirectly" (a speaker may *imply* something); *infer* means "to draw a conclusion" (a hearer may *infer* something). Examples: John *implied* that he could samba; but when he stomped on her toes, Kathleen, his partner, *inferred* that he could not.

imprudent/impudent

Imprudent means "without judgment, forethought, or concern"; one who is *impudent* shows rash boldness and a lack of respect. Examples: It's *imprudent* to spend a lot of money when you're trying to stay within a budget. The spoiled child was *impudent* and disrespectful.

in/into

In refers to location; *into* shows movement, as in: "Ellie found the lost keys *in* the mailbox after moving *into* the guest house." Also, you don't jump *in* the shower or *in* the car; you jump *into* the shower or car — you'd slip and fall, or bump your head if you jumped *in* (within) one or the other! Of course, "jump *into* the shower" and "jump *into* the car" are slang, so you wouldn't use either in formal writing.

"in between"

It is almost always redundant to say "in between"; simply use *between*. Example: The stolen check had been hidden *between* (not *in between*) two books in the library.

incidence/incidents

Incidence is the rate of occurrence of something that happens, usually unwanted; *incidents* are occurrences or events, distinct episodes, or pieces of action. Examples:

Contra Costa County Library
Walnut Creek
9/6/2023 12:43:25 PM

- Patron Receipt -
- Charges -

ID: 21901025268768

Item: 31901044240713
Title: Clean, well-lighted sentences : a guide to
Call Number: 428.2 BELL
Due Date: 9/27/2023

Item: 31901056939509
Title: Mastering workplace skills.   Grammar fu
Call Number: 428.20246 MASTERING
Due Date: 9/27/2023

n: 31901054524873
: 101 two-letter words /
Number: 428.1 MERRITT
Due Date: 9/27/2023

1901050720947
he bugaboo review : a lighthearted guid
nber: 428.2 SOMMER
e Date: 9/27/2023

formation, library hours,
ing closures can be found
:clib.org/contact-us/,
1-800-984-4636.

The graphs show an increasing *incidence* of poverty in the past decade. There were some *incidents* of shouting on the bus last night.

incite/insight

To incite is to stir up feelings or provoke action; an *insight* is a perception or the ability to see clearly. Examples: The new law *incited* a riot. Heidi's *insight* proved to be correct.

incumbent/recumbent

Incumbent as a noun refers to one who holds a specific office; as an adjective it describes one holding office, as in "the *incumbent* governor"; it also means "imposed as an obligation or duty." *Recumbent* is similar to *accumbent*, but it can also mean "resting or idle." Examples: After his grueling day's work, Jason is *accumbent* on the sofa. It is *incumbent* upon us to help those in need. Gary has stopped cutting the lawn and is standing *recumbent* against the mower, drinking a glass of lemonade. By the way, *accumbent* is an adjective meaning "reclining or lying against something."

indispensable

Spell it *able*, not "ible." The word means "absolutely necessary or essential." Example: Christopher is *indispensable* to the organization; it wouldn't function well without him.

indolent/insolent

Indolent is an adjective that means "lazy, idle, lethargic"; *insolent* describes one who is impudent, rude, or disrespectful. Examples: Some people tend to become *indolent* on vacations, not wanting to do much except lie about and relax (perhaps while drinking **Dole** fruit juices). The **insolent** little puppy wouldn't behave, insisting on chewing on the **soles** of my new Manolos!

inequity/iniquity

Inequity is a lack of fairness or justice; an *iniquity* is a grossly immoral act. Examples: The salaries of women are less than those of men for the same job, and that's an *inequity*; some would even call it a blatant *iniquity*.

infinitives

These are the "to" form of a verb (examples: **to sing**, **to jump**, **to cry**, **to split**) and shouldn't be split, or separated, if at all possible. For example, write "Try not **to split** infinitives," rather than "Try to not split infinitives." This no longer is a hard-and-fast rule, but employ it when you can; try never **to do** it!

ingenious/ingenuous

Ingenious means "clever"; *ingenuous* means "naive, candid, or guileless." Examples: Ryland's unique idea was an *ingenious* solution, but he was so *ingenuous* that he didn't even realize his valuable contribution. (Note: These words are tricky; they sound almost the opposite of what they mean, don't they?)

inglorious/vainglorious

Inglorious means "bringing shame or dishonor"; *vainglorious* means "boastful or excessively proud." Examples: The player was *vainglorious* and haughty, but when he missed the final goal, it was an *inglorious* ending for him — and the team.

"in regards to"

This incorrectly combines the phrases *in regard to* and *as regards*. Use one or the other, or use *regarding*. Example: Rita called *regarding* (or *in regard to*) plans for the party.

"inside of"

Drop the *of*; merely say *inside*. Example: Steve kept the map *inside* (not *inside of*) the car.

integral

It's not "intregal." The word means "necessary," or "an essential part of something," just as integrity is essential to have. Example: Tom and Hank are an *integral* part of the annual gathering; the party wouldn't be the same without them.

inter/intra

Inter as a prefix means "between or among, together, or in the midst of," as in "*inter*galactic space travel." The prefix *intra* means "within or inside," as in "an *intra*venous tube feeding into one's vein."

intriguing

There's no *e* in this word; it means "secret or clandestine, often in an underhanded way," or "arousing interest or curiosity through unique or crafty means." Example: The James Bond films involve *intriguing* and mysterious plots, with unusual, clandestine adventures and gorgeous women.

invalid

The noun *invalid*, pronounced "in'-va-lid," refers to one who is incapacitated by illness or injury; the adjective, pronounced "in-val'-id," means "not legally valid," or "falsely claimed."

inveigh

To inveigh means "to protest vehemently or attack strongly with words"; it's usually followed by *against*. Example: Sonja *inveighed against* the vote by Congress. (See "ei" and "ie" section on page 201.)

inveigle

To inveigle is to lure, entice, or ensnare by artful talk or inducements. It is usually followed by *into*. Example: Joey *inveigled* me *into* buying this old clunker! (See "ei" and "ie" section on page 201.)

I *or* me — *a trick to remember when using these so you don't get stung* (W.O.)

If you're unsure whether to use *I* or *me*, *he* or *him*, *her* or *she*, *they* or *them*, etc., after a preposition when another person is also mentioned, mentally take away the other person's name and hear how it sounds: "She read the map to Aaron and *I*" or "...to Aaron and *me*"? Remove the words *Aaron and*. Would you say: "She read the map to *me*" or "...to *I*"? *Me* is correct; it's not "Aaron and *I*." However, when the pronoun's the subject of a sentence, always use *I*. Examples: Marti and *I* like to dance. Graciella and *I* will go. Isabelle and *I* want to leave early.

"irregardless"

"Irregardless" isn't a word; instead, use *regardless*.

irrelevant

It ends in *ant*, like the *irrelevant* little vermin the ant.

irresistible

It's spelled *ible*, not "able." The word means "extremely tempting or enticing, or not capable of being resisted." Example: Denise's homemade cookies are **irresistible**; we look forward to savoring and devouring them each Christmas!

"I see what you're saying"

You *hear*, or you **understand**, what I'm saying, so avoid the phrase "I *see* what you're saying" — unless the words are in a cartoon bubble above the speaker's head!...or you're using sign language.

"is...is"

Don't use this word twice as a verb in the same sentence. Instead of writing, "The problem is, is that we missed the bus" or "What it is, though, is the fact that you were late," reconstruct the sentence to say, "The fact **is** that you were late" or "The problem **is** that we missed the bus."

"is when," "is where"

These constructions are excessive. It's better to say, "An extemporaneous speech **is given** with little preparation," and not: "An extemporaneous speech *is when* someone speaks without having had much time to prepare." Don't say, "On the beach is where you can often find shells"; instead say, "You can often find shells on the beach."

its/it's (W.O.)

Its, which has no apostrophe, is a possessive pronoun showing that something owns something; **it's = it is**. The apostrophe in **it's** indicates that the letter *i* has been omitted; the apostrophe does not show possession.

Examples: *It's* time to plant the rosebush; *its* petals are beginning to droop. *It's-It*, the favorite Bay Area ice-cream-and-cookie concoction, is aptly named; it's so enticing that we want to exclaim, "*It is it*; the best!"

jibe/jive

To jibe means "to be in accord with, to agree"; it also means "to taunt or make heckling remarks," and it is a nautical term for shifting sails. *Jive* is a term for jazz or swing music and the jargon of jazz enthusiasts; the verb form means "to play or dance to jive music." As slang, the noun form means "deceptive or phony talk." Examples: Your answers don't *jibe* with mine. The jazz quartet *jived* past midnight in the New York club.

kaleidoscope, kaleidoscopic

A *kaleidoscope* is a tube with angular mirrors and bits of glass at one end that together make various designs when the tube is rotated. *Kaleidoscopic* meaning changing, complex, varying, as in the changing patterns of a *kaleidoscope*. (See "ei" and "ie" section on page 201.)

"keep on"

No need to add the *on*. For example, say, "*keep* going" or "*keep* trying," not "*keep on* going" or "*keep on* trying." (One possible exception to this is the famous old expression "Keep on truckin'" — but only if you're using it as jargon or quoting it!)

"kind of/sort of," "kinda"

In formal writing, don't use *kind of* to mean "somewhat," or *sort of* to mean "rather" — and it's never "*kinda*." Use *rather* or *somewhat* instead.

"kind of a"

When you're using **kind of** to mean "type of," don't follow it with an *a* or *an*. Example: What **kind of** (not *kind of a*) pie will Stephanie order?

knowledgeable

Knowledge and **able** appear in this word.

"landed up"

This is incorrect; it combines **ended up** with **landed**. The correct phrase is **landed** or **ended up** though it's colloquial and not to be used in formal writing. Example: We **ended up** (or **landed**) in jail after crashing into the fire hydrant.

"later on"

Just say **later**; "later on" is incorrect, unless you add a comma and a prepositional phrase, as in this context: "Later, on another station, I heard 'Rhapsody in Blue.' "

lay/lie (W.O.)

To lay is to place something or put something down and must be followed by a noun or pronoun, a thing; **to lie** is to recline. A **lie** is an untruth, and **to lie** also means "to tell an untruth." Examples: Why don't you **lie** here and take a short nap? Don't **lie** to me, young man! Please **lay** your gift on the table near the others. (Hint: <u>La</u>y rhymes with p<u>la</u>ce; <u>li</u>e rhymes with rec<u>li</u>ne. But be careful: **lay** is also the past tense of the verb **to lie**, as in: "Gabriella **lay** on the couch yesterday, totally exhausted.")

lead/led

Lead (pronounced "led") as a noun refers to a type of metal; **led** is the past tense of the verb **to lead** (pronounced "leed"). Examples: Wesley *led* me to the treasure, which, in reality, was gilded *lead*!

leaped/leapt

Either of these is correct as the past participle of the verb *to leap*, which means "to spring or jump upward, or to act impulsively." Examples: Kate *leapt* (or *leaped*) at the chance to speak at graduation. Desmond *leaped* (or *leapt*) from the skiff as it edged toward the pier.

leave/let, leave alone/let alone

To leave means "to exit" or "to permit," so don't say, "*Leave* me help you." *To leave alone* is to depart from or cause to be in solitude; *to let alone* means "to not disturb." Examples: Mom told you to *let* me *alone*; I'm studying. I opened the door and saw that she was asleep, so I decided to *leave* her *alone*. I had to *leave* my injured friend alone while I went to get help. (Note: The expression "let *alone*," as in: "Genevieve doesn't have time to read fitness magazines, *let alone* buy a subscription for one," is colloquial only.)

leisure

Leisure is a time of relaxation, of freedom from the demands of work. (See "ei" and "ie" section on page 201.)

leitmotif

A *leitmotif* (pronounced "lite'-mo-tif") is a theme, or motif, that runs throughout a literary or musical work. (See "ei" and "ie" section on page 201.)

lend/loan

Both **lend** and **loan** refer to the act of letting someone temporarily borrow money or other physical property with the understanding that it or its equivalent will be returned, as. in: "Will you please **lend** me your car?" If the thing *given* is not literal or physical, use **lend**: "His presence **lends** credibility to the rally." A **loan** is a sum of money that has been **lent** ("I repaid the **loan** to the bank"); the verb **to loan** means "to make a **loan**."

lessen/lesson

To lessen is a verb meaning "to reduce, diminish, or decrease"; **lesson** is a noun, and it refers to something that is taught. (Hint: Work **on** your vocabulary less**on**.) Examples: It will **lessen** your anxiety if you learn the **lesson** to begin your projects earlier.

liable/likely

Liable means "obligated or responsible"; don't use it to mean "likely." Examples: You're **likely** (not *liable*) to stumble if you don't watch where you're going. The rental agreement stated that clients were **liable** for any damages done to the property.

license

To remember to use *c* rather than *s* my dad used to say, "Think **li**k**ense**." This works because the *c* is sometimes pronounced as a *k*.

lichen/liken

These sound the same, but **lichen** is a plantlike organism made up of a fungus and an alga, while **to liken** means "to compare or to show as similar." Examples: *Lichen* grows on the trees; it is a pesky organism, but it is so beautiful that we could *liken* it to frost.

lightening/lightning

Lightening, a verb, is the act of making something lighter in color or weight, and it has three syllables. *Lightning* is a weather-related phenomenon; it has no *e*, and it's made up of two syllables. Examples: *Lightning* struck just as Ani was *lightening* her jeans with bleach.

REPETITIOUS, EXCESSIVE, SUPERFLUOUS, UNNECESSARY, VERBOSE, AND DUPLICATE PHRASES

Avoid these (and other) redundancies:

advance planning	Jewish rabbi
and also	lie down
burn up	lift up
close down	my own personal opinion
down below	owns his own home
8:00 pm at night	raise up
fall down	refer back
free gift	staple together
funeral service	use it all up

(There are many more of these!)

"like"

Use it as a preposition or a verb, *not* as an expletive, a sentence filler. Incorrect: "I, like, don't, like, know what I'm, like, tryin' to, like, say here."

"like how"

Use "I *like the way*," rather than "I like how." Example: I *like the way* you've cut your hair this time.

loath/loathe

Loath is an adjective meaning "unwilling or reluctant"; *to loathe* is a verb meaning "to feel disgust or intense aversion for something." Examples: I am *loath* to eat lime Jell-O embedded with olives, marshmallows, and cottage cheese; I *loathe* and despise it.

loneliness

Don't forget the *e* in the first syllable.

loose/lose (W.O.)

LOOSE/LOSE

Loose is an adjective that means "not securely fastened"; *to lose* is a verb meaning "to misplace, to rid, or not to win." (Hint: *Lose* one of the *o*'s to change the word from *loose* to *lose*.) Examples: Your teeth may be knocked *loose* if you *lose* the fight.

lots/lots of

Don't use these in formal writing; they're colloquial. Instead use *many*, *much*, or, less preferable, *a lot*.

luxuriant/luxurious

These words are similar in meaning. *Luxuriant* describes abundance in growth, but it can also mean the same as *luxurious*, which describes something full of luxury. Examples: After it had been fertilized, the bush was *luxuriant* and full of blossoms. The wealthy prince's palace was indeed *luxurious*, with columns of gold throughout and *luxuriant*, healthy plants in the formal garden.

magnate/magnet

A *magnate* is an influential person, usually in business; a *magnet* is an electromagnetic object that attracts iron, or it is a person or object that attracts something else. Examples: The shipping *magnate* owned a fleet of large vessels in Hong Kong. Kaitlyn is like a *magnet*; she attracts others to her.

main/mane

Main is an adjective that means "important" or "principal"; *mane* refers to the long hair on the heads and necks of certain mammals (horse, lion) and long hair on human heads. Examples: The *main* reason Hillary cut her hair short is that it felt like a long *mane* and bothered her in the summer heat.

maintenance

Not spelled with "<u>tain</u>" as in main<u>tain</u>; the word **ten** appears in it.

maneuver

It's spelled with **eu** (although in the Harry Potter series and in other British works it's spelled "manoeuver").

manner/manners/manor

Manner is the way in which something is done; **manners** are social behaviors; a **manor** is a house and the land surrounding it. "To the **manner** born" is a phrase that means one is naturally adapted to something as though accustomed to it from birth. Examples: Misuzu takes on challenges in a determined **manner**. Laurel's **manners** are impeccable and socially perfect. The lord of the **manor** looked into every detail of the large home and its land.

mantel/mantle

A **mantel** is a shelf above a fireplace; a **mantle** is a cloak or covering. Examples: Sara put the <u>tele</u>phone on the **man<u>tel</u>**. The little trick-or-treater wore a ghostly **mantle** on Halloween. The earth's **mantle** is the layer between its crust and the core.

many/much

Use **many** to describe the quantity of things countable (good luck charms, rainstorms, dollars); use **much** to describe the quantity of things that are generally uncountable (luck, rain, wealth).

marriage

It has an *i* and the word *age* at the end — so does *carriage*.

marshal/Marshall

To marshal is a verb meaning "to gather"; *marshal* is also used as a title of a military officer, an officer of a U.S. judicial district court, in law enforcement, or the like. *Marshall* is a proper noun, a name. Examples: The fire *marshal* will *marshal* his volunteers to douse the flames. In history class, we studied the *Marshall* Plan.

material/materiel

Material is matter or substance used in making items; *materiel* refers to military supplies, weapons, or equipment. Examples: The *materials* used for the toy boat were plastic, resin, and wire. The flatbed truck carried *materiel* to the army's base camp.

may be/maybe

May be shows possibility, as in: "This *may be* Taylor's best performance ever" or "If it begins to snow, it *may be* that I'll need to leave early." *Maybe* is an adverb meaning "perhaps" and denotes a choice, as in: "*Maybe* Kaila will serve lasagna at her party, or *maybe* she'll serve spaghetti" and "*Maybe* the rain will stop, so tomorrow *may be* a brighter day." (Here's a trick for determining which spelling you need: If you can take out the *maybe* or *may be* and the sentence still makes sense, then use *maybe*, not *may be*.)

medal/meddle, metal/mettle

A *medal* is a badge or a medallion; *to meddle* means "to become involved in another's affairs." *Metal* is a solid chemical element, an alloy; **mettle** is spirit, courage, character. Examples: Finn won a **medal** made of **metal**; it took great **mettle** to do so. Don't **meddle** in the affairs of others.

media/medium

Media is the plural of **medium**. **Medium** denotes the "middle, intermediate, or midway," as in: "I like my steaks **medium** — not rare or well done." A **medium** is a conduit through which one acts or learns, or it is a source of information, as in: "Politicians use all **media** outlets to get their message across — TV, radio, blogs, newspapers, Tweets, the Internet, and small home meetings." A **medium** is also a type of art or artist's materials, as in: "The painting was a watercolor, my favorite **medium**." The term **medium** is also used to describe a person said to be able to contact the dead: "Aunt Tillie would visit Madame Lazonga, the **medium**, to speak with her long-dead husband, Uncle Ned."

memento

Not "**momento**"; think of re*mem*ber. Example: The prom ticket was a nice **memento** of their date.

micro/macro

Micro = "small"; **macro** = "large, long, excessive."

miner/minor

A **miner** digs for valuable ore or minerals; a **minor** is one who is not legally an adult; a **minor** thing or issue is one of little significance. Examples: At the tourist camp in the Gold Country, the **miner** showed us how to pan for gold, but **minors** — at this site it was those under twelve — had to be accompanied by an adult; it was only a **minor** inconvenience, though.

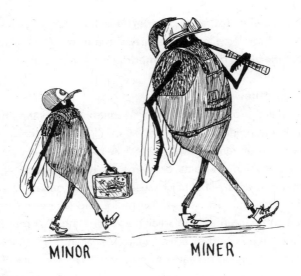

MINOR   MINER

minute

A **minute** (pronounced "min'-nit") is one-sixtieth of an hour, or sixty seconds; **minute** (pronounced "my-noot'") means "extremely small in size." Examples: Give me another **minute** to get this **minute** coffee stain off my sleeve.

mischievous

Pronounced "mis'-chi-vus." Don't say "mis-chee'-vee-us." (See "ei" and "ie" section on page 201.)

moot/mute

Moot means "arguable, open to dispute, or irrelevant," as in a "**moot** point"; **mute** ("myoot") means "unable to speak."

moral/morale

Moral (pronounced "mor'-al") relates to what is right or wrong, or to the lesson that can be learned from a story; **morale** (pronounced "mor-al'") refers to attitude, mood, or mental state. Examples: The **moral** of the story is to be kind to others. The **morale** of the team members was high because they had won the championship.

more/mores

More means "greater number, size, amount, extent, or degree"; *mores*, pronounced "mor'-ays," refers to customs or ways of doing things, especially of a society. Examples: The **more** Travis worked out, the **more** buff he became! The **mores** of society dictate that when you are in the audience of a public performance, especially one indoors, you don't talk, make unnecessary noise, eat, or disturb others — and that you turn off your cell phone! Well, okay, rock concerts are an exception!

motif/motive

A **motif** (pronounced "mo-teef' ") is a repeated theme, design, shape, or pattern; a **motive** (pronounced "mo'tiv") is the reason for doing something or behaving in a certain way. Examples: The quilt's **motif** was a series of interlocking triangles. Chuck's **motive** for working hard was to succeed in law, as his father had done.

"muchly"

Use the word **much**. "Muchly" is incorrect.

"my own personal opinion"

Who else's would it be? Omit *personal* and *own*. Example: **My opinion** is that we should leave immediately.

myself

Myself is a reflexive or an intensive pronoun, so it refers to the subject *I*. Don't use **myself** in place of *I* or **me**.

Examples: I hurt **myself**. I will plant these **myself**. Giovanni gave the cookies to Laura and me (not *myself*).

nauseated/nauseous

The distinction between these two is the same as the distinction between *sick* and *sickening*. Say that you are **nauseated** if you are ill; if you are made ill by something, that thing is **nauseous** (similar to **noxious**). Examples: Jake was **nauseated** by the **nauseous** smell of the rotting sea star.

naval/navel

Naval refers to anything nautical, maritime, or seafaring; in a less common context it means "pertaining to a navy." A **navel** is a "belly button," the point where one's umbilical cord was connected prior to birth.

necessary

Spell it with one **c** and two **s**'s.

neighbor, neighborhood, neighboring, neighborly

(See "ei" and "ie" section on page 201.)

neither/none (W.O.)

As with the word **each**, both of these are singular and traditionally take a singular verb, as in: "**Neither** (mentally add the word **one**) of the cats eats dry food," "**None** (think: 'not one') of the dolls is broken" and "**Neither** (one) of these sounds correct, but each is!" Or you can say: "These don't sound correct, but they are." (See "ei" and "ie" section on page 201.)

nevertheless

It's one word.

niece

It's pronounced "nees," but the i comes first; think of a "ni_ce **niece**."

niggardly

This word means "miserly, cheap, stingy, or parsimonious"; it has no racial connotation.

"no" *instead of* **any** *or* **a**

Don't use the word *no* to mean "any." Say: "I don't have **any** water," not: "I don't have *no* water." The second example is a double negative; it puts together two negatives, *don't* and *no*, and in English this is incorrect. And don't pair the words *not* and *no* in a double negative. Say: "I can't get **a** job," not: "I can't get *no* job." Mick Jagger notwithstanding, the sentence should be: "I can't get **any** satisfaction"!

notic_eable

Don't forget the first **e**. The word is made up of **notice** and **able**.

nuclear

Pronounce it "nu-cl_ee_-ur," not "nu-c_u_-lar"! It has **clear** in it. Example: Disasters at Fukushima, Chernobyl, and Three-Mile Island have made it clear that we should use extreme caution with **nuclear** power.

numbers

Don't start a sentence with a number, not even a date; write out the word, and don't forget to hyphenate when the number is made up of more than one word between twenty and one hundred. Examples: **Twenty-three** birds sat on the branch (not "23 birds sat on the branch"). "*Nineteen fifty-five* was a good year" (not "1955 was a good year").

object

An *object* (pronounced "ob'-ject") is a noun, an item, a perceptible thing; *to object* (pronounced "ob-ject'") is to give a dissenting or disagreeing argument, or to raise disapproval of something. Examples: Rick *objects* to dusting; it's a lot of work to clean all those small *objects*.

observance/observation

An *observance* is a celebration or special occasion; an *observation* is an inspection or a noticing of something or someone. Examples: A great *observance* of America's freedom occurs on the Fourth of July. The police department kept the suspect under close *observation*.

obst<u>a</u>cle

It's not spelled "obst<u>i</u>cle." The word is defined as "something that stands in the way or obstructs."

occu<u>r</u>, occu<u>rr</u>ed, occu<u>rr</u>ence

Remember the spellings <u>**rred**</u> and <u>**rr**</u>**ence**.

"off of"

Drop the *of* and just say *off*, as in: "I tried to get the fly *off* (not *off of*) me." Also, you don't buy something "off of" someone else; you buy it *from* someone.

WHAT A DIFFERENCE A LETTER MAKES!

To affect means "to influence."
To effect means "to bring about"; an **effect** is a result.

Aid is the act or result of helping; to **aid** is to help or furnish with assistance.
An **aide** is an assistant or helper.
AIDS is a disease of the immune system.

An **altar** is a ceremonial table.
To alter means "to change."

Apposite means "especially well suited to the circumstances."
Opposite means "facing a different direction," or "somebody or something totally different from another."

Arrant means "outrageously bad, extreme."
Errant means "wandering."

An **ascent** is an upward climb.
To assent means "to agree."

Baited is the past tense of **to bait**, meaning "to set a trap" or "to entice."
Bated means "moderated or restrained."

WHAT A DIFFERENCE A LETTER MAKES!

Bathos refers to a sudden switch from the lofty to the commonplace, an anticlimax.

Pathos is the quality of bringing forth feelings of compassion, sympathy, or pity.

To broach means "to bring up for discussion or to put forth for consideration."

A *brooch* is a large decorative pin.

To censor is to remove or suppress material considered objectionable.

A *sensor* is sensitive to light, temperature, and so on and transmits a signal to a measuring device.

To clench is to close tightly.

To clinch is to secure or settle definitely.

A *collage* is an assemblage.

A *college* is an institution that grants a bachelor's degree, or it is the undergraduate division of a university.

A *complement* is something that completes; *to complement* is to go with or complete.

To compliment means "to flatter"; a *compliment* is a flattering remark.

WHAT A DIFFERENCE A LETTER MAKES!

To deify is to make something or someone godlike.
A **deity** is a god or goddess.

Dual refers to "two, double."
A **duel** is a planned fight between two.

Elder indicates seniority or denotes one older or higher in rank.
Older means "having greater age than someone else."

To exalt means "to praise highly."
To exult means "to rejoice."

Exercise is physical activity; **to exercise** is to do physical activity or practice a skill or behavior.
To exorcise is to free someone or something from evil, or to send evil away.

Fallow means "uncultivated, unplanted."
To follow means "to come after."

A fort is a place of fortification or strength.
Forte is the French word for "strong."

WHAT A DIFFERENCE A LETTER MAKES!

Gall is bitterness or something bitter, or a skin sore caused by friction; **to gall** means "to become irritated or chafed."

Gaul is a Celt of ancient Gaul, a French person, or an ancient region in Europe.

Gauge or **gage** means "to measure" or "a standard of measurement or a device used to measure."

Gouge means "to scoop or dig out," or "to extort."

To gild is to coat with a thin layer of gold.

A **guild** is an association of people with similar interests.

Gilt is a thin layer of gold or a superficial gloss.

Guilt is being culpable for a crime or offense; the word also refers to remorse.

To hear means "to detect sound through the ear."

Here is an adverb telling where.

Heard is the past tense of **to hear**.

A **herd** is a gathering of animals; **to herd** means "to gather species into a group."

WHAT A DIFFERENCE A LETTER (OR TWO) MAKES!

Hippie refers to the flower children of the 1960s.
Hippy describes one who has large hips.

To hoard is to collect a large amount; a *hoard* is a cache saved for the future.
A *horde* is a large group of living things.

Hoarse describes a condition of the throat that makes the voice husky.
A *horse* is a four-footed animal with a mane and long tail.

Holy means "sacred"; it also refers to a divine power.
Holey describes something that is full of holes.
Wholly means "completely, entirely, or exclusively."

Indolent means "lazy, idle."
Insolent means "rude or disrespectful."

Inequity means "lack of fairness or justice."
Iniquity means "a grossly immoral act."

Ingenious means "clever."
Ingenuous means "naive or guileless."

To lessen means "to reduce or diminish."
A *lesson* is something that is taught.

WHAT A DIFFERENCE A LETTER MAKES!

A **miner** is one who digs for valuable ore.
A **minor** is one who is not legally an adult.

Naval refers to anything nautical or maritime.
A **navel** is a belly button.

To pray means "to speak to God or another deity."
Prey is the victim of a predator; **to prey** means "to victimize."

Prescribe means "to recommend a particular course of action."
Proscribe means "to ban, outlaw, or condemn something considered undesirable."

A **prophecy** is a prediction or foretelling.
To prophesy means "to foretell."

Serge is a kind of fabric with crisscrossed weave.
A **surge** is forceful movement forward; **to surge** means "to lunge or lurch forward."

To sew means "to join or repair using a needle and thread."
To sow means "to plant or scatter seeds."

WHAT A DIFFERENCE A LETTER MAKES!

Spacious means "large or great in extent."
Specious means "having a ring of truth, but in reality false."

Stationary means "unable to move."
Stationery is special paper.

A **team** is an organized group of people or animals.
To teem means "to abound in or have much or many of."

A **track** is a path or course taken; a mark left by a person, animal, or thing; or a measure of recorded input.
A **tract** is an expanse of land or water.

Vain means "holding undue high regard for oneself."
A **vein** is a blood vessel or a mineral deposit.

Veracious means "truthful, honest."
Voracious means "starving, hungry; insatiable."

A **vertex** is the highest point of something, the apex.
A **vortex** is a whirling mass.

A **vice** is a negative habit.
A **vise** is a tool with a closable jaw for holding objects.

OK, O.K., okay

Don't use these in formal writing, but in informal writing each spelling is acceptable.

onomatopo<u>ei</u>a

Onomatopoeia is the use of words that sound like what they signify, such as *bark, meow, hiss*. (See "ei" and "ie" section on page 201.)

opt<u>i</u>mistic

Hint: *Tim* is op*t<u>im</u>istic*!

oral/verbal

The word *oral* means "spoken aloud" and is also used in reference to the mouth; *verbal* means "consisting of, or in the form of, words," as in "*verbal* imagery," or "expressed in spoken words." Examples: Children learn to give *oral* reports in the second grade. The *verbal* portion of the final, the vocabulary section, is on the last page.

ordinance/ordnance

An *ordinance* is a law, rule, or regulation, especially imposed by a city or state; *ordnance* is military materiel, or the branch of the military that procures and cares for weapons, ammunition, vehicles, and so forth. Examples: The *ordinance* posted on the sign stated that civilians must stay away from the military's *ordnance*, as it sits on restricted property.

"orientate," "orientated"

"Orient<u>ate</u>" and "orient<u>ated</u>" are not standard words; use *orient* and *oriented*. Examples: Come early to *orient* (not *orientate*) yourself. The map was **oriented** correctly, so we found our bearings.

oscillate/osculate

To oscillate is to swing between two points with a rhythmic motion; **to osculate** is to kiss. Examples: We were mesmerized as we watched the sprinkler **oscillate** over the immense, verdant lawn. Young lovers tend to **osculate** a lot; kissing is natural when people are in love!

paid

The past tense of **to pay** is **paid**, not **payed**.

palatable/palpable

Palatable means "flavorful or acceptable to the taste, or agreeable to the mind or senses." **Palpable** means "tangible, capable of being touched or felt, or easily perceived." Examples: The tiramisu was so **palatable** that we all said *bravo* to Chef Luiggi. As Christina finished singing Puccini's aria, an emotional wave swept through the concert hall; esteem for her and the music was **palpable**.

palate/pallet/palette

The **palate** is the roof of the mouth or one's sense of taste; a **pallet** is a small, makeshift bed, usually wooden, with straw; it's also a temporary loading or storage platform or a flat-bladed tool used in art; a **palette** is a painter's paint-mixing board. (Hint: The word **ate** is in **pal<u>ate</u>**.) Examples: When it came to wine, Larry had a discriminating **palate**. Picasso mixed paints on his **palette**. In big-box stores and warehouses, personnel use forklifts to move **pallets** stacked high with goods.

pam**ph**let

panic**k**ing, picnic**k**ing

Add a *k* to *panic* or *picnic* when you're either *panic**k**ing* or *picnic**k**ing*! Same with *picknic**k**ed* and *picknic**k**er*. Example: Ants and bugs are consummate *picnickers*!

panino/panini

If you're going to use foreign words, use them correctly. A *panino* is one sandwich; *panini* is the word for more than one. Examples: For lunch I had a grilled ham and cheese *panino*; Teri and Jamilla had *panini* as well.

paradigm/paragon

A *paradigm* (pronounced "pair'-a-dime") is a pattern or example; a *paragon* is a standard of perfection, a benchmark. Examples: Wind energy is a *paradigm* of our efforts to reduce our dependence on fossil fuels. The winner of the spelling bee is a *paragon* among those who can spell.

para**ll**el

Notice that it has a pair of *l*'s — which happen to be *parallel* — and then a single one at the end.

parameter/perimeter

A *parameter* is a fact or factor that limits what can be done, or how; a *perimeter* is a boundary that surrounds and encloses an area. Examples: One *parameter* we must think about for this project is cost; we cannot go over budget. The chain-link fence denotes the *perimeter* of the football field.

parity/parody

Parity signifies equality in amount, status, or character; a *parody* is a humorous imitation of a serious work or person. Examples: Imagine a world in which *parity* exists among all people. *The Simpsons* is a *parody* of real-life situations.

party/person

A *party* is a group or a festive occasion; a *person* is an individual. Examples: There were seven in their *party* for dinner, but only one *person* had arrived by seven o'clock.

passed/past (W.O.)

Passed is the past (!) tense of the verb *to pass*; *past*, an adjective, means "belonging to a former time" or "beyond a time or place." *Past* can also be a noun or a preposition. Examples: Robin *passed* the pizza to me. Our *past* president spoke at the garden club. The hotel is just *past* the fountain. His *past* finally caught up with him.

pastime

It's spelled with one *s* and one *t*.

patience/patients

Patience is the endurance of pain, difficulty, provocation, or annoyance; *patients* are those receiving medical care, treatment, or attention. Examples: It takes a lot of *patience* for doctors to care for all their *patients*.

pedal/peddle/petal

A *pedal* is a foot-operated lever on a bike, car, or other machine; to *peddle* is to sell; a *petal* is part of a flower.

Examples: Bill tried to *peddle* that car to Pam, but its gas *pedal* was broken. Karen bought that dress because it is the color of yellow rose *petals*.

PETAL / PEDAL / PEDDLE

peer/pier

A *peer* is a person on equal standing with another; the verb *to peer* means "to stare or gaze intently and with difficulty." A *pier* is a platform extending from shore to water where boats dock. Examples: Teens often are influenced by their *peers*. My *peers* and I were standing on the *pier*; we were *peering* toward the horizon to catch a glimpse of the dolphins.

peignoir

Peignoir is a French word for a woman's fancy dressing gown. (See "ei" and "ie" section on page 201.)

pejorative

It begins with *pej*; it's not spelled "perjorative." A *pejorative* is a word or expression that, as an adjective, expresses criticism or disapproval; as a noun, it denotes a word or expression that disparages, criticizes, or belittles. Example: Hurling a *pejorative*, Eleanor lambasted the opposing pitcher.

percent/per cent/percentage

Percent and *per cent* (both spellings are okay to use) are always used with a specific number; *percentage* is used with a descriptive term, such as large or small. Examples: Haggai won 80 *percent* of the vote but only a small *percentage* of the electorate went to the polls.

percept/precept

A *percept*, or *perception*, is the object of something perceived by the senses; that is, one has been made aware of it. A *precept* is a law or command stating a particular course of action. Examples: Granny's aching bones provide a *perception* that it will rain soon, and the clouds above confirm that idea. Kari and I had a *percept* of something looming above us, but it turned out to be a green kite tangled in a tree. In the theater, there is an unwritten *precept* that the audience will not talk.

perform, performance

These are not spelled "preform" — and the end of the second one is spelled *ance*.

STINK BUGS! WHICH ENDING IS IT?

Watch the endings of these:

credible
eligible
irresistible
permissible

creditable
indispensable
inevitable
noticeable

guidance
hindrance
maintenance
perseverance

audience
existence
occurrence
precedence
preference
sentence

brilliant
irrelevant
reluctant

---

permissible

It's spelled with *ible*.

perpetrate/perpetuate

To perpetrate is to commit an act or to be responsible for something, usually something criminally wrong; to **perpetuate** is to make something continue for a long time. Examples: Johan **perpetrated** a rumor about his good friend, and Liza will **perpetuate** that piece of gossip for a long time by repeating it to everyone she knows.

perquisite/prerequisite

A **perquisite**, also known as a "perk," is a customary tip, an expected right. A **prerequisite** is something required in order for something else to happen. Examples: A college degree is a **prerequisite** for getting this job. The executive expected the **perquisite** of free parking in her own space.

persecute/prosecute

To persecute is to mistreat or harass, or to subject someone or a race or group of people to cruel and unfair treatment; **to prosecute** means "to take legal action against." Examples: Some insensitive upperclassmen **persecute** and bully incoming freshmen. The sign warned that the store would **prosecute** shoplifters to the full extent of the law.

perseverance

Don't add an extra *r*, — it's not spelled "perserverance." Notice that the end is spelled *ance*.

personal/personnel

Personal means "private"; **personnel** are people working at a certain job. Examples: No **personnel** of the XYZ Company may leave early for **personal** reasons.

persuade/peruse/pursue

To persuade means "to successfully convince or urge someone to do something"; **to peruse** something is to scan, read, or examine it carefully; **to pursue** is to chase or follow someone or something in hopes of catching him or her or it. Examples: Raul tried to **persuade** Franz not to **pursue** his dream of joining the circus. Linda will **peruse** her poetry book to find the perfect poem to present to her friend.

phenomenon

The plural is **phenomena**. **Phenomenon** means "something or someone out of the ordinary." Example: The extravagant opening ceremony of the Beijing Olympics was a true **phenomenon**; the world watched it, completely transfixed by its complexity and beauty.

physically

Don't spell it "physicly."

plain/plane

Plain is an adjective meaning "simple, unadorned, and easily seen," as in "in **plain** sight." It's also a noun denoting wide open space, as in a famous line from *My Fair Lady*: "The rain in Spain stays mainly on the **plain**." **Plane** is the shortened version of the word **airplane**. (Hint: A **plane** stays in a flight **lane** in the sky.) **Plane** also is a verb meaning "to make level, flat, smooth," as in: "Kile will **plane** that stair so it's smooth."

playwright

Spelled **playwright**, not "playwrite" (though isn't that what they do, write?).

plus

Plus should not be used to join independent clauses. Example: This raincoat is dirty; **furthermore** (not *plus*), it has a hole in it.

poinsettia

This plant is prevalent during the winter holidays. Pronounce the ending "tee-ah."

poor/pore/pour

Poor means "without resources" or "of inferior quality." A *pore* is a tiny opening in the skin, and **to pore** (usually used with **over**) means "to study something carefully." **To pour** is to make something flow from a vessel (a pitcher, pail, bucket, glass). Examples: The student was **poor** and had to **pour** hot water into her cup instead of coffee, as she **pored over** her homework. The new lotion promised to cleanse the skin's **pores**. This is a **poor** interpretation of the original.

portentous/pretentious

Portentous (careful: it's not "portentious") means "ominous or prodigious." "A major earthquake near the sea is **portentous**; it's likely that a damaging tsunami will follow." The word also shares one definition with **pretentious**: "showing unspecific significance, hubris, or pomposity." **Pretentious** also means "characterized by exaggerated importance or by ostentation, or by the pretense that one is more than one actually is." Examples: The phony countess was so **pretentious** that her charade was **portentous**; snooty and feigning aristocracy, she was definitely headed for a fall from grace.

possession, possessive

Double sets of *s*'s in each.

possessive pronouns and apostrophes (W.O.)

These are pronouns that show ownership, and they do not have apostrophes: *theirs, yours, ours, hers, his, its.* This may seem odd because possessive nouns *must* have apostrophes, as in: *Pablo's* scooter, the *dog's* collar, *children's* dreams, *parents'* home.

pray/prey

To pray is to speak to God or another deity; **prey**, as a noun, means "victim of a predator"; the verb **to prey** means "to victimize" (**to prey upon**).

precede/proceed

To precede is to come before; **to proceed** is to go forward; the noun **proceeds** signifies the amount of money left after all expenses for an event have been paid. Examples: As we **proceeded** up the hill, we saw footprints that indicated others had **preceded** us. All the **proceeds** from the fund-raiser went to charity.

precedence

The vowels are all *e's.* **Precedence** is the act or fact of preceding or coming before.

predominant/predominate

Predominant is an adjective that means "having power, influence, or dominion over others"; **to predominate** is a verb meaning "to be the stronger leading element or person." Examples: The gray male is the alpha wolf, the **predominant** one; he tends to **predominate** over all the others in the pack.

preference

Another word in which all the vowels are *e*'s. *Preference* is the act of setting or holding something before or above another by one's own estimation.

preferred

Two *r*'s in the second syllable.

prejudice

No *d* in the first syllable, and the word ends in *ice*. As a noun, *prejudice* is an opinion formed beforehand (one *pre-judges* something) or an irrational dislike of someone or something; the verb *to prejudice* means "to influence someone to form an opinion, usually not a rational one, about someone or something in advance." The adjective form is *prejudiced*. Examples: Do you have a *prejudice* against my purple hair? I don't want you to *prejudice* me against the movie before I see it.

prescience, prescient

Prescience means "a knowledge of things before they happen, a foresight." (See "ei" and "ie" section on page 201.)

prescribe/proscribe, prescription/proscription

To prescribe is to recommend a particular course of action or treatment to remedy something; *to proscribe* is to ban, outlaw, or condemn something considered undesirable by those in authority. Examples: Doctors *prescribe* medications for those who need them. The FBI will *proscribe* certain fugitives and put them on the "Ten Most Wanted" list.

preview/purview

A **preview** is an opportunity to see something before others do, or it is something shown in advance; a **purview** is the scope or range of something. Examples: Easton watched the **preview** of the film last night at a special showing. Plans for the new project, from the buildings to the last parking place, were under Egan's **purview**.

principal/principle

The **princi<u>pal</u>**, a noun, is your **pal** who runs the school; a **principal** is also a sum of money; as an adjective, **principal** means "most important." **Princi<u>ple</u>** is a noun meaning "a basic truth or law." Examples: The **principal** commended the students for three **principal** reasons. We believe in the **principle** of equal justice for all.

PRINCIPLE / PRINCIPAL

privilege

No *a* and no *d*.

prodigy/progeny/protégé

A *prodigy* is a person who is excellent at doing something at a very early age; *progeny* are the offspring of people, plants, or animals; a *protégé* is youngster who receives help, guidance, or financial support from an older, more experienced person (the spelling *protégée* denotes a woman). Examples: Many who attend the Marin School of the Arts were *prodigies*; they were talented at a young age, and still are. We all are *progeny* of our parents. The well-known painter took on a *protégé* in order to further expand the boy's talent.

produce/product

The noun *produce* means "raw material, plants, crops, harvest, or yield"; the verb *to produce* means "to manufacture something." A *product* is something that has been manufactured. Examples: Food companies manufacture and *produce* cuisine to be sold; some use organically grown *produce* to make healthful *products* that are entire meals or desserts.

pronouns in unnecessary places

In the following contexts, don't insert a pronoun (see "The Parts of Speech" near the beginning of the book). Don't say: "My father, _he_ likes to read Hemingway" or "Malia, _she_ works hard in school" or "The parrot, _it_ sings 'We Will Rock You!'" Simply say: "My father likes..." or "Malia works..." or "The parrot sings..."

THEY'RE NOT "BUG SPOTS," THEY'RE APOSTROPHES!

Possessive nouns must have apostrophes. Use them with the following:

the Barsottis'	parents'
children's	Spencer's
the dog's	team's

Possessive pronouns do not have apostrophes:

hers	ours
his	theirs
its	yours

propensity/propinquity

Propensity is an inclination or a tendency; a *propinquity* is a nearness or proximity, or a similarity in nature. Examples: Dani has a *propensity* for spending her entire paycheck on shoes. A *propinquity* exists among many animals; they share a kind of kinship unknown to humans.

prophecy/prophesy

Prophecy (the ending is pronounced "see") is a noun meaning "a prediction or foretelling"; *prophesy* (the ending is pronounced "sigh") is a verb meaning "to foretell."

Examples: He will give a **prophecy**, and will **prophesy** the end of the plague. (Note: "Prophe<u>size</u>" is incorrect.)

prostate/prostrate

The **prostate** is a gland found only in males. **To prostrate** means "to bow very low to the ground, bending from the waist" (the adjective form is **prostrating**), or "to lie flat in humility" (the adjective form is **prostrate**). Examples: Nate and Tate each have a **prostate**. The loyal subjects lay **prostrate** before the king.

prot<u>ei</u>n

(See "ei" and "ie" section on page 201.)

province/Providence

A **province** is a territory governed by a political or royal administration; **province** also is the range of one's proper duties, jurisdiction, or responsibilities. The word **Providence**, capitalized, means "divine guidance"; not capitalized, it denotes care and prudence in management. Examples: King Louie and Queen Michele ruled the **province** to the south of Fauxville; to the north, her royal highness Queen Sonja's **province** and authority extended to the edge of Darkling Forest. Managing all the functions of life requires **providence** and foresight — a little **Providence** from a higher power helps a lot, too!

psyche/psychic

The verb **to psyche** (pronounced "sike") means "to work oneself up emotionally," or "to analyze." **Psyche**, as a noun (pronounced "sy'-kee"), refers to the spirit or soul. A **psychic** is a person who is said to respond to or be affected by metaphysical forces — for example, a fortune-teller or a medium. Examples: The team was **psyched** for the game. Carlyle's **psyche** presented her as a happy peson because she was in love. Madam Garbonzo, the **psychic**, foretold that I would visit Dubai, and three weeks later, I did just that!

punitive/putative

Punitive describes something or someone inflicting, or wanting to inflict, punishment; **putative** means "generally accepted or presumed, supposed, reputed." Examples: He was so angry that he became **punitive** toward his dog, wanting to punish it for chewing his favorite slipper; however, the **putative** opinion about that is that it's better to teach than to punish.

qualitative/quantitative

Qualitative is related to or based on the quality or character of something; **quantitative** is related to quantity or the number of something. (Note: It's not spelled "quantitive"; you need the **ta**.) Examples: Vicki offered a **qualitative** analysis of the compound and determined that its structure was sound. Then she gave the **quantitative** report the committee requested: 240 members attended the meeting and $2,400 in dues was collected.

quay

This word, oddly, is pronounced "key." A **quay** is a wharf where a ship's cargo is loaded and unloaded.

quiet/quite/quit

Quiet means "placid, peaceful, not noisy"; **quite** means "completely, wholly, entirely"; **to quit** is to stop, end, or leave. Examples: Are you **quite** sure that Will has **quit** playing his drums and all will be **quiet** again?

quizzes

Be careful of the double *z*; it can be pu**zz**ling!

QUIZZES

quote/quotation

Quote is a verb; **quotation** is a noun. Don't use **quote** as a shortened form of the noun **quotation**. Examples: The **quotation** (not *quote*) she used from Shakespeare's play is famous. Can you **quote** it for me?

rack/wrack

The noun **rack** is a device used to hold items, such as a coatrack, hat rack, gun rack; **racked** describes something beleaguered, tortured, or stretched (this meaning is derived from the old instrument of torture called "the rack"). **Wrack** is destruction, ruin, or something that's been turned to wreckage. (Hint: **Wreck** and **wrack** both begin with **w**, which will help you to remember the difference between **wrack** and **rack**.) Examples: Harrison's job was so stressful that he was **racked** with anxiety, knowing he faced **wrack** and ruin if he were fired.

raise/rays/raze/rise

To raise, meaning "to move or cause to go upward," is a transitive verb, so a direct object (a noun or pronoun) must follow it. *Rays* are beams that project from a source, as in **rays** of light. *To raze* is to destroy or tear down a structure. *To rise* means "to go up" and is intransitive, so it doesn't take a direct object. Examples: Jaden **raised** the bar to a higher level. Sunbeams are lovely **rays** of light. The demolition company **razed** the building to the ground. Heat will **rise**.

rappel/repel

To rappel is to go down a steep, vertical face of something, using a rope that is secured at the top; *to repel* is to resist attack or keep something away. Examples: Mountain climbers **rappel** down mountainsides after climbing to their destinations. In summer, we try to **repel** the mosquitoes and other bugs.

rapprochement/reproach

Rapprochement is a resumption of friendly relations between previously estranged nations or people; it has nothing to do with the verb *to reproach*, which means "to criticize someone for doing something wrong." Examples: *Rapprochement* was finally achieved when leaders of the two countries sat down to talk meaningfully. Miguel will *reproach* you if you return the car with no gas in it.

rapt/wrapped

Rapt means "engrossed, captivated, spellbound"; *wrapped* describes something that has been enveloped or bound with paper, ribbon, a fabric, or the like. Examples: Little toddlers stared with *rapt* attention at the glittering fireworks. The mummy had lain embalmed and *wrapped* for thousands of years.

rarefied

It's not spelled "rarified." *Rarefied* means "something out of the ordinary." Example: The *rarefied* company of former presidents is shared by few.

ravage/ravenous/ravish

To ravage means "to damage or destroy"; to be *ravenous* is to be extremely hungry. *To ravish* has a more lusty meaning: "to carry off or to overwhelm emotionally." (Also, slinky black dresses and ball gowns can make one look *ravishing*!) Examples: They feared that the cyclone would *ravage* the town. The swimmers, Amber and Caroline, were *ravenous* after their long swim meet. Rhett Butler *ravished* Scarlett O'Hara in one scene of *Gone with the Wind*, carrying her up the long, sweeping stairway.

real/really

Real is an adjective and modifies a noun or pronoun; *really* is an adverb and modifies a verb, an adjective, or another adverb. Examples: The *real* truth (noun) is that

Eugenia was *really* angry (adjective)! (Note: The word *really* really should not be used in formal writing!)

Real**t**or

Don't add an extra *a*; it's not spelled "Real-<u>a</u>-tor." It's capitalized because it's a trademarked name.

"the reason...is because"

Use the word *that* instead of *because*. Example: *The reason* I'm late *is that* (not *is because*) my car broke down.

rec**ei**pt

A *receipt* is a confirmation for something purchased or for work done. (See "ei" and "ie" section on page 201.)

re**c**o**mm**end

One *c* and two *m*'s.

redundancies to avoid

The following phrases are redundant; that is, they repeat themselves, so don't use them: *Easter Sunday*, *owns his own home*, *down below*, *close down*, *burn up*, *Jewish rabbi*, *8:00 p.m. at night*, *lift up*, *raise up*, *fall down*, *staple together* — among many others.

refereeing/referring

Refereeing is the present participle of the verb *to referee*, and it means "supervising a game or sport"; *referring* means "directing to a resource for assistance or information."

reference, referral, referred

Watch how many *r*'s you use, after the first one, in each word.

regimen/regiment

A **regimen** is a recommended program of diet, exercise, or other measures that is followed rigorously, intended to improve health or fitness; a **regiment** is a permanent military unit or other large, orderly group. Examples: The team followed a strict **regimen** of diet and exercise. The **regiment** was based at Fort Hood.

reign/rein

To reign means "to rule over a population"; as a noun, **reign** denotes the length of time someone ruled, as in: "Queen Amanda's **reign** lasted twenty years." A **rein** is a leather strap fastened to either end of a bit (the portion of a bridle that fits in the mouth of a horse or other animal) and is used to control the animal. (See "ei" and "ie" section on page 201.)

relation/relationship

Relation describes a connection with *things*; **relationship** is a connection among *people*. Examples: The **relation** between job and family can be difficult to balance, but Ashley does it very well. Those sailing on the *Semester at Sea* student shipboard program had developed a close **relationship**. (Note: Those related to you are *relatives*, not *relations*.)

reluctant/reticent

Not wanting to *act* is to be **reluctant**; not wanting to *talk* is to be **reticent**. (Hint: **Reluctant** ends in <u>ant</u> and relates to <u>act</u>, both of which start with **a**.) Examples: Ken was nervous and **reluctant** to go to the party, but he had been **reticent** in communicating that to his pals, so they didn't know.

rep<u>eti</u>tion

respectfully/respectively

Respectfully means "showing or marked by respect"; **respectively** means "each in the order given." Examples: I **respectfully** disagree with you. Francesco, Marta, and Diego were a dentist, an architect, and a surgeon, **respectively**.

restaur<u>ate</u>ur

No *n* — the word is not spelled "restaura<u>n</u>teur." Example: One who runs a restaurant is a **restaurateur**.

RESTAURATEUR

resume/résumé

To resume means "to begin or take up again after a pause." A *résumé* (pronounced "re'-zu-may" — we often omit the accent marks in English) is a brief account of one's personal, educational, and professional qualifications and experience, used in applying for a job. Examples: The race will *resume* after the dangerous oil slick is cleaned up. After graduation, students prepare a *résumé* to begin their careers.

reveille

Reveille (pronounced rev'-il-ee) is the musical signal — usually by bugle or drum — used to awaken or assemble military personnel (or camp kids!). (See "ei" and "ie" section on page 201.)

reward/reword

A *reward* is something given or received in return for service; the verb *to reward* signifies the act of giving a reward. *To reword* is to put into other words, to paraphrase. Examples: Ruthi got a *reward* for solving the puzzle. Please *reword* this statement so it's in plain English!

rhythm, rhythmical

Odd spellings; watch the *h*'s.

ridiculous

It's spelled *rid* — not "red." It means "absurd, preposterous, or deserving ridicule."

rife/ripe

The term *rife with* means "occurring everywhere in great supply." Don't incorrectly substitute the term *ripe*. *Ripe* means "ready and pleasant to eat." Examples: The trees were *rife* with fragrant blossoms. Those peaches look luscious and *ripe*; let's sit down right now and devour them!

TO *OR WITH OR* FOR *OR* ON *— WHICH TO USE?* IT'S AN ITCHY PROBLEM

Use the correct preposition with the following terms:

To agree to means "to give consent to."
To agree with means "to be in accord with or to come to an understanding with."

To compare to means "to represent as similar two things of different class."
To compare with means "to examine the ways in which two things of the same class are similar."

To differ from means "to be unlike."
To differ with means "to disagree with."

To talk to is used when the other person or thing isn't talking or doesn't talk.
To talk with is used when the other is responding to you.

To wait for means "to be in readiness for or to await."
To wait on means "to serve."

right/rite/wright/write

Right means "correct or proper," or it signifies the opposite side of "left" (as in: "**right** shoe" and "left shoe"). It also refers to something that a person has a legal claim to. A *rite* is a passage or ritual or ceremonial act. A **wright** is a person who builds or creates something; this term is most often used in compound words, such as *playwright* and *shipwright*. *To write* means "to inscribe or record." Examples: Fedor owns the **rights** to the song. Vanessa stood by her son's side during the ceremonial **rite** of passage. Ashlyn will **write** to her mom.

roommate

This word is spelled with two *m*'s. **Roommates** are two or more people who share a room. (Think: two people = two *m*'s.)

root/rout/route

A *root* (sounds like boot) is the normally underground part of a plant that draws nutrients and water from the soil; it is also an essential part or element, as in "the **root** of the issue," or the primary source, mainly of a family. The verb *to root* means "to dig in the earth or rummage for something, or to give audible encouragement or applause to a contestant or team": "Lexi led the cheerleaders in encouraging the crowd to **root** for the team." *To rout* (sounds like out) is to defeat overwhelmingly (a *rout* is an overwhelming defeat), as in: "The Hornets will **rout** the Mustangs in the final game; the score will be lopsided, just watch and see!" *Rout* also means "to dig through or up," as in *routing* through old papers or *routing* in the ground with a trowel. A *route* (pronounced either "root" or "rowt") is a road, highway, or course of travel from one place to another. The verb **to route** means "to send or schedule something to be delivered by a specific means or path." Examples: Some know the wonderful old song "Get Your Kicks on **Route** 66"; today that term has been reenergized with the electronics term **router**, and its pronunciation has changed. Can you have Gwen **route** this through to Seattle for me, please?

run amok

Run amok is the preferred spelling of this term, not "run amuck." It means "to get wild and crazy"! Example: Taytum and Kunal tend to **run amok** when finals have finished!

sacrifice

The vowel in the middle syllable is *i* not *a*. The word is not spelled "sacrafice."

sandwich

Don't forget the **d**, and don't add a *t*. It's not spelled "sandwitch" or "sanwich" or "samwich."

sari/sorry

A **sari** is the classic, draped woman's garment of India and Pakistan; **sorry** is a feeling or saying of regret, sadness, or sympathy. Examples: "I'm **sorry** I stepped on your beautiful **sari**, Zaida!"

Satan/satin

Satan is a name for the devil, who is considered to be the evil adversary of God and the leader of the fallen angels; **satin** is a smooth fabric with a shiny face and dull back.

schedule

It's pronounced "sked-jewel," at least in the US.

science

(See "ei" and "ie" section on page 201.)

seamen/semen

Seamen are men who go to sea, such as mariners or sailors; *semen* is the secretion of the male reproductive organ.

seismic, seismological, seismologist, seismology, seismograph

Seismic, which is the root word for the other terms in this list, means "pertaining to, of the nature of, or caused by an earthquake"; it also can refer to something else that seems "earthshaking." Example: A *seismic* event occurred in Berlin: as the entire world watched, residents ripped out the hated wall that had snaked through that beautiful city and divided it. (See "ei" and "ie" section on page 201.)

seize, seizure

To seize means "to take hold of suddenly or forcibly." (See "ei" and "ie" section on page 201.)

sensual/sensuous

Sensual means "preoccupied with the gratification of the senses" or "carnal, voluptuous, lusty, kinky, lewd, or unchaste" (the meaning of *sensual* is similar to that of *sexual*). *Sensuous* means "pleasing to or pertaining to or felt through the senses," especially in reference to art, music, and nature. Examples: The voluptuous and often lusty tango is a dance that can be classified as *sensual*. A trip to the museum can be a *sensuous* excursion when you view all the inspiring paintings; it is especially true if you eat in the outdoor garden café, where classical music is playing and the magnolias are in bloom.

sent<u>e</u>nce

Not spelled "sent<u>a</u>nce" — the word *ten* is in it.

sep<u>arate</u> (W.O.)

There's *a rat* in sep<u>arat</u>e. It's not spelled "sep<u>e</u>rate."

serge/surge

Serge is a kind of twilled, worsted, or woolen fabric, or another fabric with a twill (meaning "somewhat criss-crossed") weave. The verb *to surge* means "to lunge or lurch forward," while the noun *surge* signifies a force-ful movement forward. Examples: The gentleman wore a blue *serge* suit. The crowd *surged* onto the field after the team's victory.

s<u>e</u>rgeant

It's not spelled "s<u>a</u>rgeant," though it sounds as if it should be. A *sergeant* is a noncommissioned officer in the U.S. military.

set/sit

To set, as a transitive verb, must have an object follow-ing it; in this context it means "to place something" (as in: "Janice has *set* the vase on the windowsill"). *To set* also means "to put something in a specified state or place" ("Tarah, please *set* the table for dinner"). As an intransi-tive verb, with no object following, *to set* means "to be-come firm or harden" ("The cement has *set*"). *Set* is also a noun meaning "a unit or collection" ("Use the good **set** of glasses"). Or it refers to the location of a TV show or movie ("Quiet on the **set**"). **Sit** is a verb that signifies a person's act of positioning his or her bottom upon a resting place ("Tell Nicco to **sit** here while I find the papers").

sewing/sowing

Sewing is the act of joining things, or repairing objects, using a needle and thread; **sowing** describes the act of planting or scattering seeds. Examples: Stefany began **sewing** the costumes for the school production. The botany club members were **sowing** vegetable seeds in order to have carrots and lettuce by spring.

SOWING

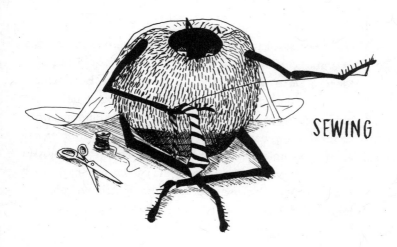

SEWING

sheik or sheikh

A *sheikh* (or *sheik*) is the male leader of a tribe, village, or religious body (in Arab and other Muslim use). (See "ei" and "ie" section on page 201.)

shining

It has only one *n* in the first syllable — the long *i* sound signals that only one consonant should follow it. The same is true of *dining, lining, mining, pining, whining.*

shone/shown

Shone is the past tense of the intransitive verb *to shine* (intransitive means the verb has no object following it). *Shown* is the past participle (that is, it uses *has, had,* or *have* as part of the verb) of the verb *to show.* Examples: The moon *shone* on the placid lake like a beacon. The book *had shown* me the way to achieve inner peace at times when I needed it most. (Note: The past tense of the transitive verb *to shine* is *shined,* and it has an object following it, as in: "Jiang *shined* his shoes before the wedding.")

since

Don't use *since* to mean "because" if there is any chance of ambiguity (a double meaning), as there is in this sentence: "*Since* we won the match we have been enjoying ice cream floats." In this case, *since* could mean either "because" or "from that time"; use a different word to make the meaning clear, such as *when* or *after* or *because.* Examples: *When* we won the match we enjoyed ice cream floats. *After* we won the match we enjoyed ice cream floats. *Because* we won the match we enjoyed ice cream floats.

skein

A **skein** is a length of yarn or thread wound around a reel or object for easy use. (See "ei" and "ie" section on page 201.)

skillful

Two *l*'s in the center, one at the end.

sleigh

A **sleigh** is a light vehicle on runners that is drawn by an animal over snow or ice. (See "ei" and "ie" section on page 201.)

sleight/slight

Sleight means "skill or dexterity"; it also can mean "trickery or cunning." **Slight** means "very small in degree, amount, importance, or size"; it can also mean "to snub or ignore." As a noun, a **slight** is an "affront or insult." Examples: The **slight** girl was short in stature, but large in caring. It is unkind to **slight** another person's accomplishments. Charlie the magician used **sleight** of hand to make the beautiful woman disappear. (See "ei" and "ie" section on page 201.)

smell

Be careful of using the word **smell** when you mean that something "has an aroma or odor"; if you say, "The lettuce **smells**," it could mean that the lettuce is capable of discerning odors. Instead, say, "This lettuce **smells** rotten" or "This lettuce has a terrible odor."

sneaked

The word is **sneaked**, not "*snuck.*" Examples: We **sneaked** past the sleeping dog and into the haunted house. "*Snuck*" has **sneaked** into everyday usage, but it's not preferred by those in the know!

so

When you use **so** in a sentence — and you're not using it as a conjunction — it must be followed by the comparison word **that**, unless it's an expression of excitement, which must usually be followed by an exclamation point (!). Examples: Lacey was **so** small **that** she shopped in the kids' department. I'm **so** excited about this news!

society, societies

(See "ei" and "ie" section on page 201.)

sole/soul

Sole means "single, only one." **Sole** also refers to the bottom surface of a foot or shoe, and it's a kind of fish. **Soul** refers to the spiritual part of a person. Examples: Delaney was the **sole** responder to the question; nobody else even ventured a guess. There was a hole in the **sole** of Mondee's shoe. We ordered sautéed fillet of **sole**. Mrs. Kincaid is a kindly person with a good **soul**.

soliloquy

The ending is odd: **quy**. A **soliloquy** is the act of speaking onstage as if alone — even though others too may be onstage at the moment — that lets the audience know the character's thoughts.

DON'T GET STUNG BY THESE!

Be sure to use the correct word:

Between/among
Use **between** when referring to two items or people.
Use **among** when referring to three or more.

Good/well
Good is an adjective that describes a noun or pronoun.
Well is an adverb and modifies a verb, an adjective, or another adverb.

If/whether
Use **if** to express a condition.
Use **whether** to express alternatives — but don't use "whether or not" in most instances.

In/into
In refers to location.
Into shows movement.

Lay/lie
To lay is to put down or place something, and it must be followed by a noun.
To lie is to recline or to tell an untruth; a **lie** is an untruth.

somebody, someone, sometime, something

These terms are pronouns and are almost always written as one word; the few exceptions depend on the context of the sentence.

someday, somehow, someplace, sometime, sometimes, somewhat, somewhere

These words are adverbs (remember, adverbs tell how, when, where, why, under what conditions, or to what degree); these terms refer to *unspecified* descriptions and are spelled as one word. Examples: **Somebody** ate the cookies. **Someday** we will return. I put it **somewhere**. (In these examples, we're not certain who or when or where, so this is left unspecified.)

sooth/soothe

Sooth (sounds like "tooth") is archaic for the words *truth* and *reality*; **to soothe** (sounds like "smooth") is a verb meaning "to pacify or calm, or to ease pain." Example: Let me **soothe** that wound for you.

sovereign, sovereignty

Sovereign denotes a monarch or ruler with supreme power, or it is an adjective describing that power. Example: Queen Marina has **sovereign** power. **Sovereignty** is supremacy of authority or rule as exercised by a **sovereign** or **sovereign** state, or by power, authority, or royal rank. Example: The elite group of intellectuals claimed **sovereignty** over the large window table at the Roastery each morning. (See "ei" and "ie" section on page 201.)

spacious/specious

Spacious means "large or great in extent." *Specious* (pronounced "speeshis") describes something that has a ring of truth but that in reality is false; it looks good or right but lacks merit and is not genuine; it's pleasing to behold, but deceptive. Examples: After Dexter furnished his **spacious** home in the hills, he learned that the carpets and art were **specious** — fakes sold by a disreputable dealer who had borrowed someone else's showroom!

spade/spayed

A **spade** is a narrow shovel used for gardening; **spades** are also a suit in cards. *Spayed* describes a female animal that has been "fixed" — has had her ovaries removed.

spec**ie**s

(See "ei" and "ie" section on page 201.)

speech

It's spelled with two *e*'s. The words *beach*, *teach*, *peach*, *reach*, and *leach* are all spelled with *ea*, but **speech** and certain other words, such as *beech* (the tree) and *leech* (the bloodsucker), have two *e*'s.

stalactite/stalagmite

A *stalactite* is an icicle-like mineral deposit that hangs down from the roof of a cave; a *stalagmite* is a conical mineral deposit that builds up on the floor of a cavern; it's formed by the dripping mineral-rich water. (Hint: The word with the *t*, **stalactite**, grows from the <u>t</u>op of the cave; the one with the *m* builds up like a <u>m</u>ountain.)

stalk/stock

A **stalk** is the stem that supports a plant part such as a flower, flower cluster, or leaf; the verb **to stalk** means "to walk off angrily, or to move menacingly, as in tracking prey." For example: "Damian **stalked** off in a huff after we accused him of **stalking** Murray to get the secret formula!" **Stock** has several **meanings**: it refers to the total amount of goods a store has (as in: "Their **stock** of sandbags was low after the flood"); the capital, or funds, that a company raises through the sale of its shares ("My **stock** in XYZ Company has gone up since they diversified"); the trunk of a tree or a plant, or a stem, onto which another is grafted ("The **stock** of my favorite plant has grown nicely because we grafted it with a new shoot"); the raw material of which something is made (as in soup **stock**); a device for confining a person at the wrists and ankles ("Pillories and **stocks** were used on those who committed crimes in the colonial days"); and the repertoire of a theatrical company (as in summer **stock** productions).

stanch/staunch

This is interesting: **To stanch** (or **to staunch**) means "to stop the flow of a liquid or something intangible"; the adjective **staunch** (or **stanch**) describes something loyal and dependable, or strong and sturdy. So, although they have different definitions and different spellings, they seem to be interchangeable!

stationary/stationery

Stationary means "fixed in place, unable to move"; **stationery** is letterhead or other special writing paper. (Hint:

Stationery with an *e* comes with an <u>e</u>nvelope.) Examples: Evan worked out on his *stationary* bike. The duke's initials and crest appeared atop his personal *stationery*.

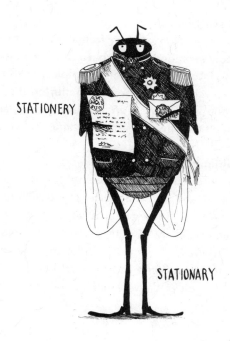

STATIONERY

STATIONARY

st<u>ei</u>n

A *stein* is a mug, usually for beer, or a measure of the quantity within it. (See "ei" and "ie" section on page 201.)

straight/strait

Straight means "not crooked, curved, or bent," or "not gay"; a *strait* is a narrow body of water that joins two larger bodies of water.

strength

It's pronounced "stre<u>ng</u>-th," not "stren-th." The **ng** is pronounced like the **ng** in stri<u>ng</u>.

stuff, "and stuff like that"

Don't use **stuff** as a noun in formal writing or in decent human conversation! The verb **to stuff** means "to cram something into a tight space." Examples: **Stuff** that paper into the recycling bag, please. Ron **stuffed** the basketball through the hoop. We **stuff** the turkey at Thanksgiving. (Note: Don't use the phrase "and stuff like that" — ever!)

sublime/subliminal

Sublime is an adjective meaning "impressive in size, scope, or extent" or "magnificent"; **subliminal** is an adjective meaning "hidden, unconscious," or "thought or done unintentionally." Examples: Roger Waters's production of The Wall was fantastic and incredibly imaginative; in short, it was **sublime**. Advertisers' placement of products in films gives viewers **subliminal** messages to buy those products.

su<u>b</u>tly

The word is pronounced "suttly" or "sudtly."

suc<u>cee</u>d

It has two **c**'s and two **e**'s.

succor/sucker

Succor is relief or assistance in time of stress or distress, or one who gives assistance or relief. A **sucker** is a lollipop, candy on a stick; it is also one who is easily fooled; **to sucker** means "to trick or deceive." A secondary shoot from the roots or low on the trunk of a plant also is called a *sucker*. Examples: Mom gave *succor* to Jubilee when the mean kids pretended to give her a big, striped *sucker* and then called her a *sucker* when they ripped it away from her little hands.

sufficient

(See "ei" and "ie" section on page 201.)

supersede

Although it sounds as if the word should end in *cede* or *ceed*, it's the exception. **Supersede** means "to take the place of something older, less modern, less efficient." Example: This model of toaster **supersedes** the one sold last year.

"sure and"/sure to

Don't use *"sure and"*; use **sure to**. Example: Be **sure to** (not *sure and*) pack your toothbrush.

surfeit

A *surfeit* is an excess. (See "ei" and "ie" section on page 201.)

surveillance

Surveillance denotes a watch kept over a person, group, suspect, prisoner, or place. (See "ei" and "ie" section on page 201.)

take for granted

Don't spell the phrase this way: "*take for granite*."

talk with/talk to

Use **talk with**, unless the other person or thing doesn't talk or doesn't return the conversation. Examples: I **talked with** Megan today, as she was **talking to** her plants.

taunt/taut

To taunt is to tease, mock, goad, or insult; *taut* is an adjective meaning "stretched tight, rigid, or inflexible." Examples: Children tend to *taunt* pigeons by running after them and scaring them. The yacht's jib line was pulled *taut*; it was very secure.

team/teem

A *team* is an organized group of people; it can also refer to animals, as in "a *team* of horses"; *to teem* means "to abound in or have much or many of." Examples: The *team* played ball in the old field, which was *teeming* with weeds; it hadn't been cared for in months.

tear/tier

A *tear* (rhymes with "*ear*") is a drop of the salty liquid that lubricates the eye, or that appears when we cry; the verb *to tear* (pronounced "tair") means "to rip apart or separate roughly." A *tier* (also rhymes with "*ear*") is one of a series of steps, rows, or ranks lying one above another. Examples: A *tear* definitely will flow if Alice *tears* her gown by catching the hem on one of her high heels — especially if she's near the three-*tiered* wedding cake!

temperature

It's spelled and pronounced "tem-per-a-ture" (not "tem-pe-ture"). Example: The *temperature* is higher today than it was yesterday. (Note: Temperatures get higher and lower, not warmer and cooler.)

tenet/tenant

A *tenet* is a belief, opinion, or doctrine; a *tenant* is someone who pays to live in, or operate a business in, a building

owned by someone else; as a verb it means "to occupy another's land." Examples: A **tenet** of the club was that it's
important to support education, so they have a fundraiser
every year. Arlene and Barb were **tenants** in my building and lived upstairs.

tenor

The word **tenor** has two meanings, and it is pronounced
the same way in each case. It denotes the higher register of a male singing voice or musical instrument; it can
also mean "the course of thought or meaning that runs
through something written or spoken." Examples: Luciano
Pavarotti was a famous opera **tenor**. The **tenor** of Lena's
argument was that there is too much government involve-
ment; she said it again and again.

than

Here's a trick that will help when you're confused about
which pronoun to use following the word **than**: "She is older
than me"? or "She is older **than I**"? Add the understood
verb and see how it sounds. Would you say: "She is older
than I am" or "She is older **than me am**"? The answer: **I**,
of course. Examples: They are happier **than we** (not **us**) are.
Miles is taller **than I** (am). (Remember: It's not all right to
skirt this issue by using *myself*; see the entry for *myself*).

than/then (W.O.)

Than is a conjunction used in comparisons; **then** is an adverb denoting time. Examples: I think this is more trouble
than it's worth, but let me see it again in a while; **then** I'll
decide.

that/which/who

That and *which*, although most often used to refer to things, may be used to refer to a group or class of people, but not to an individual; use *who* instead. Examples: Michael wondered how a woman *who* (not *that* or *which*) wore such high heels could walk on the runway, though hers were the shoes *that* looked the most beautiful, he had to admit.

that *and* which *clauses*

If you can drop a clause beginning with *that* or *which* and not lose the point of the sentence, use *which*; if not, use *that*. Also, a "which" clause has to be enclosed in commas; a "that" clause doesn't. Examples: Paul's bulldog, *which* had one white ear, won best in show. The dog *that* won best in show was Paul's bulldog.

"the both of you"

Merely say *both of you*. Example: Why don't *both of you* (not *the both of you*) join us for dinner?

th<u>ei</u>r/there/they're (W.O.)

Their is a possessive pronoun, as in: "It's *their* turn to pay." *There* is an adverb specifying place, or where something is located. (Hint: *Here* and *there* both speak of place, and the word *here* actually appears inside the word *th<u>ere</u>*.) *There* is also an expletive (a meaningless word), as in: "See *there*? I told you that would happen!" It is also an interjection, something that shows feelings or emotion: "*There*! That's finished!" *They're* is a contraction of *they are*, as in: "*They're* happy to see you." (A contraction is a combination of words, with an apostrophe ['] in place of a missing letter or letters.) (See "ei" and "ie" section on page 201.)

th<u>ei</u>sm, th<u>ei</u>stic

The root word of **theism** means "a belief in one God as the ruler and creator of the universe." (See "ei" and "ie" section on page 201.)

themselves

Use **themselves**, not "*theirselves.*" Example: Rosie and Chris treated **themselves** to ice cream after painting the patio.

there are/there's (W.O.)

Be sure that the noun that follows **there's** is singular, not plural, as in: "Look! **There's** a bird" or "**There's** a problem here." Do *not* say, "*There's* a lot of problems today" or "*There's* a lot of people here." When the noun that follows is plural, use **there are**, as in: "**There are** a lot of people here." To check whether this is correct, say simply: "**People are** here."

this

Be specific; don't write: "We were walking on *this* dark road when *this* big dog jumped out at us!" Instead, use *a*, *an*, or *the* — unless you are pointing to the exact road and the specific dog. Examples: Winnie and Marika were walking down **the** dark road when *a* big dog appeared. As we walked down **the** road, **this** dog that I'm holding by the collar jumped at us.

threw/through (W.O.)

Threw is the past tense of the verb **to throw**; **through** is a preposition, or an adverb meaning "in at one side, end, or surface and out the other" or "to the end." Examples: **Through** her binoculars, she saw who **threw** the rock that morning. I'm just passing **through** Hawaii on my way to visit Japan.

THREW

THROUGH

throes/throws

Throes is a noun meaning "a violent convulsion or struggle"; *throws* is the present tense of the verb *to throw*; a *throw* is a coverlet. Examples: So, Meredith is in the *throes* of a sneezing attack, when funny old Mack *throws* an entire box of tissues to her! She put the *throw* over her feet to keep them warm.

throne/thrown

A *throne* is a noun denoting an extravagant chair upon which royalty sits; *thrown* is the past participle of the verb *to throw*. Examples: Queen Isabella sat on her *throne*, listening to Christopher Columbus. I could have *thrown* the ball farther if I hadn't been so tired.

'til/till/until

'Til and **until** mean "to the time of," but if you use *'til*, be sure to include the apostrophe [']. Also, don't add the word *up* before any of these — don't say: "It was light *up* until the time she left" or "*Up 'til* then she was my friend." The verb **to till** means "to prepare the soil for crops"; as a noun, **till** denotes a box or drawer for holding money. Examples: Bruce went out to the pasture to **till** the soil. The shopkeeper put the cash into the **till**. Connie was afraid of the dark **until** she was four years old. Stella said she'd love Arlo **'til** the end of time.

timber/timbre

Timber refers to standing trees or their wood; *timbre* (pronounced "tambr") is the tone or color of a musical or vocal note or sound. Examples: Some say we are decimating the forests by using too much **timber**. The **timbre** of the baritone's voice was rich and deep.

to/too/two (W.O.)

To is a preposition (always followed by a noun or pronoun) meaning "a direction toward a point"; it's also part of the infinitive, or basic form, of a verb (for example, **to sing**, **to love**, **to ask**). *Too* is an adverb meaning "also or in addition" or "more than is desirable." (Think: The extra **o** is **too** many!) *Two* is the number just past *one*. Examples: **Bungee jumping** is fun **to do**. Those who find it **too** scary, go **to** the ice cream store instead and get a **two**-scoop cone!

tortuous/torturous

Tortuous means "crooked, winding, and full of turns"; *torturous* means "painful" (it comes from the word **torture**). Examples: As Jose hurtled through the air on the fair's **tortuous** loop-de-loop, he developed a **torturous** headache.

toward/towards

These words are interchangeable, although **toward** is preferred in the United States. The same is true of *backward*, *forward*, *afterward*, *upward*, *downward*, and *onward*. In each case, it's best to leave off the *s*.

track/tract

A **track** is a mark left by a person, animal, or thing; it's also a path or course taken, or a measure of recorded input, as in "soundtrack." A **tract** is usually an expanse of land or water. Examples: The **track** was soggy for the runners after the rain. The land was used for **tract** housing after the developer bought it.

traffi<u>c</u>

No *k* at the end.

tra<u>g</u>edy

There's no *d* in the first syllable.

CONTRACTIONS

These are combined words with missing letters. For example:

I'm = I am
it's = it is
they're = they are

we're = we are
who's = who is
you're = you are

transferred
Notice the two **r**'s that appear together in the last syllable.

tries
The word is not spelled "trys."

truly
Not spelled "truely."

try to, sure to
Don't use "*try and*" or "*sure and.*" Use **to** instead of *and*, as in: "***Try to*** (not *try and*) remember her birthday" or "Be ***sure to*** (not *sure and*) send a card." If, however, the word ***try*** is followed by the conjunction and in a sentence that has a compound verb (two verbs), this combination is correct, as in: "Hiroshi will ***try and*** she will win."

Tudor/tutor
Tudor refers to the royal house of Tudor, or persons or characteristics of the period (1485–1603) when the Tudors reigned in Britain; a ***tutor*** is a personal instructor or a teacher who gives additional academic coaching.

unanimous

unnecessarily
The word has two **n**'s and two **s**'s.

until
It's not spelled "untill."

up

Don't use *up* as a verb in formal writing or dialogue; use **raise**. Example: Stores tend to **raise** (not *up*) the prices just before a sale.

us

The pronoun **us** is not used as a subject, so you cannot start a sentence with "*Us* boys" or "*Us* kids"; say it this way instead: "**We** boys" or "**We** kids." To check yourself, mentally remove the word following *us* and hear how it sounds. For example, if you're wondering whether it's correct to say, "*Us* boys like to eat," try saying it this way: "*Us* like to eat," which, of course, is incorrect.

usage

Don't spell it "useage" — and don't employ it when the word **use** will do. Example: **Use** of the school copier increases in the week leading to finals. The international greeting of *ciao* is a **usage** borrowed from Italian.

used to, supposed to

These phrases require the **d**. Don't use "use to" or "suppose to."

utilize

It means "to make use of" but it can sound pretentious. In place of "We *utilized* the best workers," it's better to say: "We **used** the best workers."

vacuum

Yes, it has two **u**'s. The same is true of *continuum*.

vain/vane/vein

Vain means "holding undue high regard for oneself" or "valueless or fruitless," as in: "She tries in **vain** to be happy." A **vane** is an object used to show which way the wind blows. A **vein** is a blood vessel or a mineral deposit. Examples: The **vain**, pompous miner cut his wrist **vein** on the sharp weather **vane** and dropped blood on the gold he'd mined from his rich mineral **vein**.

veil

A **veil** is used to hide or cover something. (See "ei" and "ie" section on page 201.)

veracious/voracious

Veracious means "truthful, honest"; *voracious* means "starving, hungry; insatiable." Examples: Matt has always been **veracious** and truthful — important qualities in a friend. After the marathon, the runners were **voracious**, eating everything in sight!

vertex/vortex

A **vertex** is the highest point of something, the apex; a **vortex** is a whirling mass, as of water, air, or fire, or a confused and whirling state of affairs or violent activity. Examples: Trent has reached the **vertex** of his career; he is the CEO of his own large company. The tornado created a **vortex** of whirling air and rain — and mass confusion.

veteran/veterinarian

A **veteran** is one who has served in the military, or who is highly experienced in something; a **veterinarian** is one who practices the medical or surgical care of animals (in informal language, both are referred to as "vets"). Examples: We honor our **veterans** with a special day in the fall. The **veterinarian** was able to put a tiny splint on Kelly's leg, and my funny little parrot will be fine, now!

via

Via means "by way of" and does not refer to the method of conveyance one uses — and it doesn't mean "by means of." For example, it's correct to say, "We drove home **via** the old road." It's *not* correct to say, "We drove home *via* car" or "Gloria gave me the message *via* Joshua."

vice/vise

A **vice** is a negative habit; a **vise** is a tool with a closable jaw for holding objects. Examples: Her **vice** is telling fibs, and her friends don't trust her now. He used a **vise** to glue the two parts of the broken box. (Note: Both words are pronounced the same.)

vill**ain**

Spelling hint: The **vill*ain*** had ***lain*** in wait for his victims.

waist/waste

The **waist** is the part of the body just above the hips; **waste** is material that is unused or useless; the verb **to waste** means "to lose through inaction or to wear away and decay." Examples: Her **waist** began to grow as her pregnancy proceeded. His muscles started to **waste** away when he became a couch potato. All that paper is **waste**, and we don't need it; please recycle it.

wait for/wait on

Wait for means "to be in readiness for or to await"; *wait on* means "to serve." Examples: We're **waiting for** (not *waiting on*) Allison to take us to the opera. The waitress **waited on** us, taking our order courteously.

waive/wave

To waive is to give up or relinquish. *To wave* is to move something back and forth; a **wave** is the movement in a body of water. Examples: Mary **waived** her right to a hearing. Let's **wave** hello to the incoming canoe passengers who are riding that **wave** to the shore.

wander/wonder

To wander is to move about without definite purpose or objective, or to roam or walk aimlessly. *To wonder* is to think about or to speculate curiously. Examples: Sometimes I **wonder** about life as I **wander** along a quiet, pristine path. (Think: "w**a**nder **a**round" — both contain the letter **a**.)

wanton/wonton

Wanton is an adjective meaning "lewd or immoral"; **wonton** is a delicious kind of stuffed Chinese noodle.

ware/wear/where

The word **ware** refers to a product that is sold, such as an item of clothing; **to wear** is a verb meaning "to have on or to carry on one's body." **Where** is an adverb meaning "in or at what place." (Hint: The word **here** is inside it.

Where? *Here!*) Examples: *Where* shall I *wear* the *wares* that I just bought on sale?

WARE / WEAR / WHERE

wary/weary

Wary is an adjective meaning "cautious, suspicious, or guarded"; *weary* means "tired, fatigued, or worn down." Examples: Johanna was *wary* of the news he had given her; she didn't quite believe it. The nation's people were *weary* of being at war.

"ways"

This word is nonstandard and colloquial when used to speak of distance. Use: "It was a long *way* (not a long *ways*) from here." Do, however, use **ways** as the plural of the noun **way**, meaning "method," as in: "There are many **ways** to trim the budget."

weather/whether

Weather deals with atmospheric conditions; **whether** is a conjunction used to introduce one of two or more alternatives. (Spelling hint: **We**ather has **w** for *west*, and **e** for *east* in it — the **weather** in the east and the west.) Also, in most instances it's not necessary to add "*or not*" when you use **whether**; the word itself implies the ambiguity of **or not**, and adding the phrase is redundant. Examples: I don't know **whether** you agree with me, but we don't want any bad **weather**, do we?

weight

(See "ei" and "ie" section on page 201.)

weird

Another weird spelling! (See "ei" and "ie" section on page 201.)

wench/winch

Wench is a slang term for a woman or girl, especially a peasant or a servant, or sometimes a wanton woman. A **winch** is a stationary machine used for hoisting or hauling, driven by either hand or motor, with a rope or chain wound around a drum and attached to the load being moved. Examples: At the Renaissance dinner, our waitress was jokingly called a serving **wench**. Catherine and Barry got blisters on their hands from using a hand-powered **winch** to haul their boat out of the muddy water!

wend/wind

To wend is a verb meaning "to go, proceed, or pursue." The verb *to wind* (pronounced "wȳned") means "to change direction or course indirectly or circuitously," or "to coil or twist around something"; it also means "to impart power to a mechanism by cranking or winding, as a clock, sometimes with a key." The noun *wind* (pronounced like "win") denotes air in natural motion. Examples: We will *wend* our way across the sand, as the *wind* blows gently across the beach. Remember to *wind* the antique clock at midnight.

were/we're

Were is the past tense of the verb *to be*; *we're* is the contraction of *we are*. (A contraction is a combination of words, with an apostrophe ['] in place of a missing letter or letters.) Examples: *We're* wondering if the river is nearby; we think we *were* given the wrong directions at the lodge.

where

Don't use *where* in place of *that* or *in which*. Examples: I heard *that* (not *where*) the crime rate is increasing. It is a story *in which* (not *where*) the children solve the mystery.

while

Avoid using *while* to mean "although" or "whereas" if it may create ambiguity or confusion — for example: "*Although* (not *while*) Sasha was enjoying the picnic, Roberto was playing a mean game of bocce ball." The two people described in this sentence may not have been eating/playing at the same time, and using *while* would make it sound as if they were.

whine/wine

To whine is to complain in a childish manner, usually in a high-pitched voice. *Wine* is an alcoholic beverage made of the fermented juice of grapes or other fruit. Examples: A sign saying "No sniveling and no *whining*" adorns the front of my classroom! The vertical *wine* tasting will resume after we cleanse our palates.

who/whom

Who is used as the subject of the verb; *whom* is used as the object of a preposition or as a direct object, as in these examples: "To *whom* (object of preposition) do we owe thanks for these hors d'oeuvres? And *who* (subject) ate all the crab puffs?" "Sam named *whom* (direct object) as the guilty one?" Think of this: *Whom* usually corresponds to someone who has been the object of an action, and *who* corresponds to the one who is doing or has done the action, as in: "An old woman, to *whom* the room had been rented, left at dawn. An old woman, *who* rented the room, left at dawn." To decide which one to use, you could also try substituting the word *him* or *her* for *whom*, and *he* or *she* for *who*, as in: "*Who* (or *whom*?) was the one who sang?" Substitute *he* or *him* for *who* or *whom*: *he* was the one or *him* was the one? The answer is *he*, so use *who*. "Laila made it for *he* or *him*?" It's *him*, so use *whom*.

"whole nother"

This is incorrect, though we hear it often. "*Nother*" isn't a word! Say: "That's *another* story altogether," not "That's a *whole nother* story."

who's/whose (W.O.)

Who's is the contraction of *who is*. (A contraction is a combination of words, with an apostrophe ['] in place of a missing letter or letters.) *Whose* is a pronoun, the possessive (showing ownership or possession) of *who*, used as an adjective. Examples: *Who's* the one who wondered *whose* shoes these were?

windy/windy/winding

Windy, pronounced "win-dee," is characterized by a lot of wind, as in "a *windy* night" or "a long *windy* speech." *Windy*, pronounced "whine-dee," is nonstandard; *winding* ("whine-ding") refers to something crooked or curving (as in "a *winding* path"), or to wrapping something around an object (as in "*winding* thread around a spool"), or to coming to a close (as in: "The summer is *winding* down").

worse/worst

Worse compares two or more items or people in regard to *bad* and *ill*; *worst* is the superlative (expressing the most by degree) of *bad* and *ill*. (*Wurst*, by the way, is a kind of sausage.) Examples: The flood was *worse* than we'd thought; in fact, it created the *worst* water damage we'd seen in decades.

writing

Spell it with only one *t*. The long vowel sound of the first *i* is followed by only one consonant — the same is true of the words *smiling, biting, shining, dining, whining,* and *lining.*

yin and yang

The term is **yin and yang**, not "ying and yang."

you

Don't use **you** in an indefinite sentence to mean **anyone**. "**Any viewer** (not you) can tell he's sincere." Also, don't use the second-person **you** in formal writing, as in: "You know that something is about to happen to Caesar because of the foreshadowing Shakespeare employs." Instead, write, "**The reader** knows..."

CHOOSE THE CORRECT BUG, ER, WORD!

Hint: These homonyms may sound the same, but spell them right when you write them.

Boer/boor
Boer relates to the Dutch colonists in South Africa.
A **boor** is a person who is rude and has little sense of decorum.

break/brake
To break is to separate or destroy.
A **brake** is what stops a vehicle.

coarse/course
Coarse means "rough in texture."
A **course** is a path or unit of study.

CHOOSE THE CORRECT BUG, ER, WORD!

cue/queue
A *cue* is a clue or a stick used for pool or billiards.
A *queue* is a line or a braid.

discrete/discreet
Discrete means "distinct, diverse."
Discreet means "judicious, prudent."

faze/phase
To faze means "to upset or disrupt the composure of someone or something."
Phase is a stage of development, or, as a verb, "to do something systematically by phases."

forbear/forebear
To forbear is to tolerate with great patience or to abstain.
A *forebear* is an ancestor.

foreword/forward
The *foreword* of a book gives introductory remarks.
Forward means "directed or moving toward the front" or "taking bold action."

gait/gate
A *gait* is a manner of walking, running, or moving along on foot.
A *gate* is a movable barrier that closes a gap in a fence or wall.

CHOOSE THE CORRECT BUG, ER, WORD!

gored/gourd
Gored usually means "pierced by an animal's horns."
Gourd is a member of the squash family.

holy/holey/wholly
Holy means "sacred" or refers to a divine power.
Holey describes something that is full of holes.
Wholly means "completely, entirely, or exclusively."

incidence/incidents
Incidence is the rate of occurrence of something that
  happens, usually unwanted.
Incidents are occurrences or events, distinct episodes, or pieces of action.

incite/insight
To incite is to stir up feelings or provoke action.
An *insight* is a perception or the ability to see clearly.

lichen/liken
Lichen is a plantlike organism made up of a fungus
  and an alga.
To *liken* means "to compare or to show as similar."

magnate/magnet
A *magnate* is an influential person, usually in business.
A *magnet* attracts iron, or it is a person or object
  that attracts something else.

CHOOSE THE CORRECT BUG, ER, WORD!

main/mane
Main means "important" or "principal."
A *mane* is the long hair on the heads and necks of certain mammals, and the long hair on human heads.

mantel/mantle
A *mantel* is a shelf above a fireplace.
A *mantle* is a cloak or covering.

plain/plane
Plain means "simple or unadorned" or "a large open space."
A *plane* is an airplane; to plane means "to make level."

sole/soul
Sole means "only one," or "the bottom of a foot or shoe," or it is a kind of fish.
Soul is the spiritual part of a person.

spade/spayed
A *spade* is a narrow shovel.
Spayed describes a neutered female animal.

throws/throes
Throws is the present tense of the verb **to throw**.
Throes means "a violent convulsion or struggle."

CHOOSE THE CORRECT BUG, ER, WORD!

to/too/two
To is a preposition.
Too is an adverb meaning "also."
Two is the number after one.

your/you're (W.O.)

Your is a possessive pronoun; *you're* is a contraction of *you are*. (A contraction is a combination of words, with an apostrophe ['] in place of a missing letter or letters.) Examples: *You're* the one who broke *your* promise.

z<u>ei</u>tg<u>ei</u>st

Another weird spelling! *Zeitgeist* means "the sense and feeling of a particular time or era." Example: Flappers, fun, and racoon coats portrayed the *zeitgeist* of the 1920s. (See "ei" and "ie" section on page 201.)

THE "EI" AND "IE" SECTION

THESE WORDS ARE JUST WAITING TO BITE YOU

I n this segment, Bug and Boo help you buzz through the vexing hornet's nest of how to spell words containing *ie* and *ei* vowels. The "*i before e except after c*" rule works minimally, but so many exceptions exist that I have categorized them in this section.

Usually in words in which *i* and *e* appear together, the order is *ie*, except when directly following the letter *c*. Here are some examples of the latter: **deceive**, **conceit**, **ceiling**. While clever sayings about how to remember the exceptions abound, many exceptions to *those* exist, so here is one main mnemonic device you may use for remembering, followed by a list of exceptions: "Use *i* before *e* except after *c* — but not when your eight veiled heirs are being weighed, or when the atheistic, feisty neighbor drinks caffeine or feigns false height, seizing the beige counterfeit sleigh and yelling (with kaleidoscope in hand), 'The heinous foreign sovereign reigns herein;

albeit not as a deity!'" On second thought, it might just be easier to memorize the exceptions than to remember this *weird* device!

Root ei *words not following* c:

atheism	heifer	reveille
beige	height	seismic
being	heinous	seize
caffeine	heir	sheikh
codeine	heist	skein
counterfeit	herein	sleigh
deify	inveigh	sovereign
deign	inveigle	stein
deity	kaleidoscope	surfeit
dreidel	leisure	surveillance
eight	neighbor	their
feign	neither	theism
feisty	onomatopoeia	veil
foreign	peignoir	vein
forfeit	protein	weight
freight	reign	weird
geisha	rein	zeitgeist

Root ie *words following* c:

ancient	financier	society
conscience	glacier	species
deficient	policies	sufficient
efficient	prescient	
fancied	science	

THE FINAL STINGERS

COMMONLY MISSPELLED WORDS

The following are commonly misspelled bugaboo words:

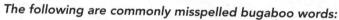

absence	aggravate	apparently
academic	all right	appearance
accidentally	almost	appropriate
accommodate	although	arctic
accomplish	altogether	argument
accumulate	always	arising
achievement	amateur	arithmetic
acknowledge	among	arrangement
acquaintance	analyze	ascend
acquire	annual	assassinate
across	answer	assess
address	apology	association

athlete

athletics

attendance

audience

bachelor

basically

beginning

believe

benefited

brilliant

Britain

bureau

buried

business

cafeteria

calendar

camaraderie

candidate

carriage

category

cemetery

changeable

changing

characteristic

chosen

column

coming

commitment

committed

committee

comparative

competitive

conceivable

conference

conferred

congratulations

conqueror

conscience

conscientious

conscious

continuum

convenient

courteous

criticism

criticize

curiosity

dealt

decision

definitely

descendant

describe

description

despair

desperate

develop

dictionary

dining

disagree

disappear

disappoint

disastrous

dissatisfied

eighth

eligible

eliminate

embarrass

eminent

emphasize

entirely

entrance

environment

equation

equivalent

especially

exaggerated

exercise

exhaust

existence

experience

explanation

extraordinary

extremely

familiar

fascinate

February

foreign

forty

fourth

friend

frustrated

fulfill

government

grammar

guard

guidance

harass

height
humorous
illiterate
imaginary
imagination
immediately
incidentally
incredible
indefinitely
indispensable
inevitable
infinite
intelligence
interesting
irrelevant
irresistible
knowledge
laboratory
legitimate
license
lightning
literature
loneliness
maintenance
maneuver
marriage
mathematics
miscellaneous
mischievous
necessary
nevertheless
niece

noticeable
obstacle
occasion
occasionally
occur
occurred
occurrence
optimistic
original
outrageous
pamphlet
parallel
particularly
pastime
perform
performance
permissible
perseverance
perspiration
phenomenon
physically
picnicking
playwright
poinsettia
politics
possession
practically
precede
precedence
preference
preferred
prejudice

preparation
prevalent
primitive
privilege
probably
proceed
professor
prominent
pronunciation
quantity
queue
quiet
quite
quizzes
Realtor
receive
recognize
recommend
reference
referred
regard
religion
repetition
restaurant
rhythm
rhythmical
ridiculous
roommate
sacrifice
sandwich
schedule
secretary

seize
separate
sergeant
several
siege
similar
sincerely
soliloquy
sophomore
specimen
strictly
subtly

succeed
superstition
surprise
suspicious
temperature
thorough
traffic
tragedy
transferred
tries
truly
unanimous

unnecessarily
until
usually
vacuum
vengeance
villain
weird
whether
writing

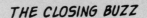

AFTERWORD

THE CLOSING BUZZ

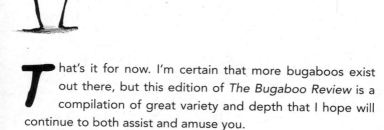

That's it for now. I'm certain that more bugaboos exist out there, but this edition of *The Bugaboo Review* is a compilation of great variety and depth that I hope will continue to both assist and amuse you.

I also know that there may be a few mildly disgruntled readers who disagree with some of the content, as well as those who are ecstatic that their nemeses have been put into a convenient, fun, and simple compilation.

Wherever you fit into the spectrum, I hope that this compendium has been of value to you.

All the best,

SUE SOMMER

ABOUT THE AUTHOR

Photo credit © Teri Williams

Sue Sommer teaches honors English and creative writing, a course she developed for Marin School of the Arts at Novato High School. Sommer leads educational tours to Europe during summers and won the Golden Bell Award for excellence in teaching in 2004. She has worked as a magazine editor and proofreader and has served on the San Francisco Recreation and Parks commission. She lives in Corte Madera, California.

Early in her first year of teaching English, Sommer realized that her students were deficient in essential grammar, spelling, and usage. She began to list "worst offenders" on the board for review and weekly quizzes. One morning she arrived at class and was shocked to find that a new janitor had erased the board clean! Thus began *The Bugaboo Review*, which you now hold in your hands.